Note:

Please note that road numbers in France are currently being modified and are subject to change.

The road numbers on the following Tours have been taken from the latest available information and are believed to be correct at the time of printing.

Distances and riding times given throughout the Tours are approximate only.

The publishers cannot accept any responsibility for any inaccuracies nor for any consequences arising from the use of these Tours, be it in respect of route numbers, accommodation details, GPS co-ordinates or any other matter.

motorbike tours of europe:

FRANCE

edition:one

European Motorbike Touring

Published by European Motorbike Touring

introduction:

This book has been written as a practical guide for motorcyclists wishing to tour France, and will be especially helpful for those that have not taken their bike abroad before.

The ten tours in this booklet all cover very different areas of France, from the rugged coastline of Brittany to the mountains in the Pyrénées, the Verdon, Tarn and Jonte Gorges in the south to the stunning châteaux in the Loire Valley, and not least of all, the rivers and woods in the Dordogne and the vineyards in Burgundy. One of the tours includes the famous 'Route Napoléon' from Grenoble to Cannes, rated by bikers throughout Europe as one of the best biking roads in France.

With a few exceptions, most of the suggested tour routes avoid motorways and instead follow selected rural 'D' roads across country. Written by a biker with years of touring experience in France, all the tours contain practical information on how to get there, where to stay, and what to do when you get there.

With helpful route notes, packing lists, touring tips, legal and ferry information, plus dozens of GPS co-ordinates and photographs related to each tour, the book is a little gem for experienced tourers and newcomers alike.

index:

tournumber:1

Cherbourg – Dinan – Cherbourg

SUMMARY
Duration: 3-4 days
Cherbourg – Dinan: 212km (131 miles)
Time: 3 hrs (riding)
Dinan – Cherbourg: 209km (130 miles)
Time: 3 hrs (riding)

TOUR OVERVIEW

The tour commences from the ferry terminal at Cherbourg in Northern France, and finishes the same day at the citadel of Dinan to the north east of Brittany, in the Côtes-d'Armor département. The ride is a distance of around 212km (131 miles), and can be completed comfortably in approximately 3 hours, although this does not take into account any stops you may make for breaks, fuel and so forth. Dinan is a lovely city and the base for the duration of the tour, with excellent places to visit and some good roads to ride on.

If you have never been to France before on your motorbike then this is the perfect tour for your first one. It's a great, leisurely introduction to North-West France that offers a surprising variety of different roads and places to visit. Navigating to Dinan and back is very straightforward. The tour is a personal favourite as you can be in a lovely region of France within 3 hours of arriving in the country, and is therefore ideal for a weekend break.

Brittany Ferries offer several options to Cherbourg from Poole, and one from Portsmouth. From Poole there is a high speed morning service from mid May to the end of September which takes just over 2 hours, or there is the normal morning service on alternate days which takes just over 4

A suggested Hotel in Dinan to stay

hours. Unless you plan on staying overnight in Cherbourg, the afternoon service from Poole is not really an option. From Portsmouth there is only the high speed option.

Personally, the option I normally take for a long weekend break is to leave Poole on a Friday morning on the normal service arriving Cherbourg early afternoon. I can then be in Dinan early in the evening and

A view from Pointe du Grouin.

enjoying dinner in a favourite restaurant within the old City walls a short time later! I normally return to Cherbourg for the early evening ferry back to Poole on the Sunday. As Cherbourg is so close to Dinan it means you can leave your departure from the town until after lunch if you wish.

ROUTE DESCRIPTION

There is nothing spectacular about this route, but it's uncomplicated and gives you a comfortable ride on good 'D' and 'N' roads through some pleasant countryside. If this is your first ride in France then it's a perfect introduction to get you familiarised and used to French speed limits and signage etc.

Just over half of the route follows the coastline down the western side of the Cherbourg peninsula to Avranches. Even without Sat/Nav, navigation is easy. Just follow the signs for the towns of Les Pieux, Barneville-Carteret, Lessay, Coutances, Granville and Avranches in that order, and all should be fine!

The route takes you around the town of Coutances, but if you have the time it's well worth diverting off into the centre. On the town's summit is the Cathédrale de Notre-Dame (**GPS:** N49.04773 W1.44483), visible throughout the surrounding countryside, and it is quite spectacular. On leaving the town make sure you come out on the D971 signposted Granville / Avranches.

At Avranches join the main N175 dual carriageway heading southbound (Rennes, St-Malo, Le Mont-St-Michel). After about 8km (5 miles) the road leads straight onto the start of the A84 motorway, which you don't want to take. Ensure you stay on the N175 by bearing off to the right where it's signposted St-Malo / Le Mont-St-Michel.

Once on the St-Malo, Le Mont-St-Michel, Dinan part of the N175 (becoming the N176) dual carriageway, it's straightforward all the way to the Dinan exit.

The return journey back to the Cherbourg Ferry Terminal is the reverse of the route down.

WHAT TO DO WHEN YOU GET THERE

There is much to see and do in the area, not least of all in Dinan itself. Here are a few favoured places and routes to do.

Dinan

Dinan is located on the western banks of the River Rance, where most of the town is encircled by almost 3km of medieval walls that remain virtually intact throughout. Within the walls are numerous medieval houses and cobbled streets, tempting crêperies, cafés and attractive shops. The church of St-Sauveur (**GPS:** N48.45361 W2.04202) is the town's main focus located near the walls to the east. Well worth a visit is the lovely Port du Dinan, and the best and most interesting way to get there is to walk down the very steep and cobbled rue du Jerzual, out through the medieval gates onto the rue du Petit-Fort arriving at the River Rance and Port du Dinan at the bottom (**GPS:** N48.45636 W2.03835). Cafés and crêperies abound along the river bank, and you can hire small motorboats by the hour to spend time on the river and get a real appreciation of Dinan's fortifications.

St-Malo

Located some 25km (16 miles) to the north of Dinan at the mouth of the Rance is the coastal town of St-Malo, and of special interest is the old citadelle which makes it the most visited place in Brittany. On a motorbike the more interesting way to ride to St-Malo from Dinan is via Dinard. Take the N176 heading east and leave at the next junction onto the D766 then D266 to Dinard. From here St-Malo is well signposted and a short distance across the River Rance. Once within the old city walls (**GPS:** N48.65087 W2.02659 on the seafront is as good as anywhere to aim for) you will find a maze of cobbled streets, with numerous hotels, cafés, restaurants, shops etc. It is always lively and often crowded, especially during the holiday season. There are some very good beaches just outside the ramparts that

The harbour at Cancale

you can walk along, which are worth a visit, as is a walk out to the small island of Grand-Bé at low tide if you have the time.

Cancale

If you like eating oysters (huîtres) then you have to go to Cancale. This small, but very pretty port, is famous for its oysters, and at low tide you can see where they are grown. Along the port area (**GPS:** **N48.67115 W1.85363**) facing the sea are many fine fish restaurants offering oysters, mussels (moules marinières) and fish soup (soupe de poissons). Parking for bikes along here is very good, even in the holiday season. The prettiest way to get to Cancale from Dinan is to go to St-Malo first (see above) and come out of the town on the coastal road, the D201, to Pointe du Grouin to the east, and thence on to Cancale a few km to the south. This road has some fine coastal views, and a visit to the windswept Pointe de Grouin (**GPS:** **N48.70827 W1.84523**), where there is a good car park for bikes, to see the rocks and, on a good day, views of

Port du Dinan

Mont St-Michel, is worth the effort. A very pleasant route back to Dinan from Cancale is to come out on the D76 southbound for a short distance to Les Portes Rouges. At the crossroads (traffic lights) turn left onto the D155 coastal road turning right at Le Vivier-sur-Mer to Dol-de-Bretagne. At Dol

Outside the old citadelle of St-Malo

take the N176 dual carriageway back to Dinan if you are pushed for time, or go into the attractive town first, the main high street starts at **GPS:** N48.54957 W1.75590, and then out on the D676 then D795 to Dinan. The approximate round distance from Dinan - Dinard - St-Malo – Pointe de Grouin – Cancale – Dol-de-Bretagne – Dinan (via the D676/795) is 88km (55 miles).

Mont St-Michel

Mont St-Michel, (**GPS:** N48.63502 W1.51066), which has ceased to be an island as the causeway leading to it no longer gets submerged, is the site of a stunningly beautiful high-spired Abbey. It is amazing to look at, even more so the closer you get to it. If you have not been there before then this is a 'must' visit. Apart from the Abbey there are some pretty, narrow streets with plenty of shops, bars, cafés and restaurants. The car parks to the south-east of the causeway are huge, and parking the bike is not an issue. The best place to put the bike is right up close to the island just past the main car park exit – you're certain to see other bikes there as well - otherwise you could have a long walk. Mont St-Michel is only just off the N176 road back to the Cherbourg ferry, so if you're catching the early evening departure stopping off here on the way is a perfect end to the tour. Directions from Dinan is either on the N176 to Pontorson then the D976 to Mont St-Michel, or come out of Dinan across the River Rance to Lanvallay and then onto the D795 / D676 to Dol-de-Bretagne to join the N176 to Pontorson then the D976.

Cap Fréhel area

Cap Fréhel is located about 40km (25 miles) north west of Dinan (**GPS:** N48.67862 W2.31811), and on a nice day this is a good ride out. Apart from going to Cap Fréhel, where there are many beaches, heathlands and views, it's convenient to visit the pretty

Mont-St-Michel

coastal villages of Sables-d'Or-les-Pins (**GPS:** N48.64106 W2.40308) and Erquy (**GPS:** N48.62914 W2.46634). If you want to make a day of it and take a circular route back to Dinan, there are several excellent roads to ride on. To get to Cap Fréhel from Dinan, head out north on the D2 to Ploubalay, then left onto the D168 before taking the D786 to Matignon. After Matignon stay on the D786 then turn right onto the D34 signposted to Pléhérel-Plage (Vieux-Bourg) and Cap Fréhel, then right again onto the D34A to the Cap. From the Cap come back along the D34A to Sables-d'Or-les-Pins where the road becomes the D34. At the 'T' junction turn right onto the D786 and shortly afterwards turn right to visit Erquy. If you intend doing the circular route back to Dinan then come out of Erquy onto the D786 becoming the D17A heading south, and just after the village of St Alban turn off left onto the D791 to Lamballe. Go through Lamballe and out on the D14 heading south. At the junction with the D792 turn right to Collinée, around the town and out on the D6 to Merdrignac. From Merdrignac take the D793 all the way back to Dinan via Broons. The circular tour is about 146km (91 miles).

Suggested Places to Stay...

HOTELS

Hôtel De La Porte Saint-Malo
35 rue Saint-Malo, 22100 Dinan
Tel: +33 (0)2 96 39 19 76
Email: info@hotelportemalo.com
Web: www.hotelportemalo.com
GPS: **N48.45799 W2.04277**

Notes: Excellent location just to the north of the old city walls. 15 rooms, from about €55. No private parking at the Hotel, but Marc (Owner) has several empty, secure garages just around the corner from the Hotel which he's happy to make available for storing motorbikes. Let him know before you arrive. He speaks fluent English and is an excellent host. Nice bedrooms. Good breakfast. No evening dinner but not a problem as the Hotel is located a mere 5 minutes from the old city walls where there are numerous restaurants and bars to choose from.

Hôtel Le Challonge
29 Place Duguesclin, 22100 Dinan
Tel: +33 (0)2 96 87 16 30
Fax: +33 (0)2 96 87 16 31
Email: lechallonge@wanadoo.fr
Web: www.hotel-dinan.fr
GPS: **N48.45121 W2.04432**

Notes: Good location on the southern outskirts of the old city walls. 18 double rooms from €53. Private parking available.

CAMPING

Camping Municipal la Hallerais
4 rue de la Robardais, 22100 Taden
Tel: +33 (0)2 96 39 15 93
Email: camping.la.hallerais@wanadoo.fr
GPS: **N48.28289 W2.01370**

Notes: 226 pitches in 6 hectares. Opening season 14th March to 1st November. Located just to the NE of Dinan.

B&B

Le Petit Châtelier
22100 St Samson sur Rance
Tel: +33 (0)2 96 39 47 89
Mobile : +33 (0)6 66 10 86 62
Email: pierette@lepetitchatelier.com
Web: http://www.lepetitchatelier.com
GPS: **N48.49944 W2.00570**

Notes: Contact Pierrette and Pascal Papail. Located approx. 5km (3 miles) north of Dinan centre. Open all year. 18th century restored farmhouse offering accommodation in a separate wing. Four rooms available comprising two doubles and two split level family rooms both with a double and two single beds. All rooms have private facilities.

Vue de la Rance
5 – 7 Rue de Grippais, La Hisse, 22100 St Sanson sur Rance
Tel: +33 (0)2 96 87 49 70
Mobile: +33 (0)6 32 59 56 42
Email: reservations@vuedelarance.com
Web: http://www.vuedelarance.co.uk
GPS: **N48.49136 W2.00574**

Notes: Contact Alison. Located approx. 5km (3 miles) north of Dinan centre. Guesthouse boasting magnificent views over the River Rance. Five guestrooms, all with modern ensuite facilities. Three doubles with one single, one double and one double with an adjoining room with two singles. Secure garage parking available.

tournumber:2

Caen – Chauvigny – Caen

SUMMARY
Duration: 3 days
Caen – Chavigny: 397km (246 miles)
Time: 6 hrs (riding)
Chavigny – Caen: 395km (245 miles)
Time: 6 hrs (riding)

TOUR OVERVIEW

This tour commences from the ferry terminal at Caen in Northern France with the aim of reaching the lovely small town of Chauvigny some 397km (246 miles) to the south the same day, staying in the town itself or nearby for two nights, before returning to Caen and the ferry back.

In addition to getting some good riding in, the principal aim of the tour is to visit the old village and unique memorial at Oradour-sur-Glane just south of Chauvigny, which became a World War II memorial village soon after the defeat of Nazi Germany in 1945.

Following the first overnight stay at Chauvigny, the second day is a short ride to Oradour, some 90km (56 miles) away to the south, returning later in the day to your accommodation in or near Chauvigny. Using the same accommodation for two nights allows you to leave your luggage/panniers behind whilst exploring the area.

Bearing in mind that Chauvigny is around 397 km (246 miles) from Caen, setting off early in the morning from the port is preferable so that you can arrive mid-afternoon, even with stops along the way. If you take the overnight ferry from Portsmouth to Caen (Ouistreham) you can be on your way soon after 06:30 hrs. To complete the whole of the return journey to Caen on the third day means a very early start in the morning in order to get to the ferry departing at 16:30 hrs, unless you decide to take an extra day out. There are many possibilities on the route back, and one suggestion is Bagnoles-de-l'Orne, about 18.6km (11.5 miles) east of Dornfront.

Chauvigny High Street – the N151 (note the Hotel on the left)

From Chauvigny, Bagnoles-de-l'Orne is around 314km (195 miles), and only 101km (63 miles) from the ferry terminal at Caen. Bagnoles is essentially a spa town for the wealthy, but it's a pleasant

The main centre at Chauvigny

place to stop overnight, and riding through the picturesque Forêt des Andaines on a sunny day is worth doing. The details of a suggested place to stay here are given at the end.

ROUTE DESCRIPTION – CAEN TO CHAUVIGNY AND ORADOUR

This is a straightforward route, fairly easy to navigate if you don't have Sat/Nav, and a good run down the central/west side of the country passing through some pleasant towns and villages on good roads. Apart from a small section towards the end of 67km (42 miles), the route avoids motorways and most dual carriageways.

Coming out of Ouistreham on the D514 towards the Caen ring road is easy, but you need to stay alert, even with Sat/Nav, and make sure you take the correct road around the city to come off at Junction 11 for the D562.

The main bridge spanning the River Vienne into Chauvigny

As you head south on the D562 you are essentially following the River Orne until just before Condé-sur-Noireau. The road from Thury-Harcourt is particularly attractive as it follows close to the river for about 11km (7 miles). Navigating from Caen until just before Mayenne is easy as you remain on the D562 throughout. If you miss the turning left for the bypass around Flers, as I often seem to do, it doesn't really matter – just head straight through the town following the signs for Domfront and you'll rejoin the D562 the other side. Flers is actually a reasonable place to stop off for a break.

The simple way to navigate through Mayenne is to follow the signs for Laval (N162). Note that shortly after leaving the town you need to take a left onto the D24. Mayenne, located in the Pays de la Loire region, straddles the River Mayenne which passes through its centre. The town itself is steeped in history. Of particular note is it's medieval castle, recently restored, and the excellent museum there. The surrounding area is also well known for its cider production. There are some pleasant cafés near the river which makes it a good place to have a break.

The D24 is a good, fast, cross country road to Montsurs, Vaiges etc., before you join the D21 then D306 and D959 to Sable-sur-Sarthe, La Flèche, le Lude and finally Tours. The final part of the D959 from Château-la-Vallière to the outskirts of Tours, some 26km (16 miles), is particularly enjoyable countryside to ride through.

Navigating around the northern part of Tours might seem daunting, but in reality all you need to do is follow the signs for Poitiers and the A10-E5 motorway. You join the A10 heading south, coming off at junction 26 to Châtellerault. it's straightforward going around the north and east of the town to get onto the D749 to Chauvigny. The D749, which follows the River Vienne through Chauvigny and then on to Lussac-les-Châteaux, is a lovely scenic ride.

Burnt out cars in Oradour

From Chauvigny to Oradour it's out heading south on the D749 to Lussac-les-Châteaux. Then it's the straight and fast N147 to the outskirts of Bellac, before turning off onto the D675 down to the tiny village of Le Chêne-Pignier. The D675 is a good road to ride on, quite fast with some nice bends, particularly where it winds through the dense forests of the Monts de Blond. At Le Chêne-Pignier turn left onto the D9 then D3 leading to Oradour, about 10km (6 miles) away.

The return route to Caen from Chauvigny is the same route as the one you came down on, mainly due to time constraints, particularly if you intend doing this over a three day period. If you are pushed for time there is of course a much faster route back once you get to Châtellerault, via the A10 to Tours, A28 to Le Mans/Alençon, the new A88 to Falaise then the N158 to Caen, but it's all motorway and dual carriageway.

Chauvigny

Chauvigny (**GPS: N46.56949 E0.64480**) is a small, pretty market town on the banks of the River Vienne. The old medieval town, which looks down on the modern part, has a collection of five medieval castles. It's worth going up there in the evening, albeit a steep climb, as there are a number of excellent restaurants to eat in. There are two weekly markets held on a Thursday and Saturday.

Oradour-sur-Glane

Oradour-sur-Glane is a small town/village in the Haute-Vienne Department of France located approximately 22km (14 miles) north-west of Limoges. The town was destroyed on Saturday 10th June 1944 by soldiers of the 2nd Waffen-SS Panzer Division Das Reich, and during the destruction that day they killed a total of 642 men, women and children.

There is to this day no clear, commonly accepted explanation as to why the SS troops acted as they did, and why Oradour was chosen for the attack. Following the massacre the town was looted and all the buildings set on fire. The following day the troops continued their journey up to northern France to assist other units of the German Army in trying to repulse the allied landings in Normandy.

After the war the French government under General Charles de Gaulle decided that the town would not be rebuilt, that it would remain as a memorial and tribute those who lost their lives on that fateful day.

Therefore the original town has been kept exactly as it was on the 10th June 1944. Visitors are free to go around the destroyed town where you will see machinery and wrecked rusting cars in the inhabitants driveways, gutted burnt buildings, old power lines and tram tracks in the streets, a small station etc., and the Church, where over 400 women and children were massacred. The village is always very quiet, and it's a moving experience to go there.

In 1999 the then French President, Jacques Chirac, dedicated a visitors' centre, the Centre de la Mémoire (**GPS: N45.92920 E1.03422**), in Oradour-sur-Glane and named the site a Village Martyr. This centre is absolutely excellent and a visit highly recommended.

For further details on Oradour go to www.oradour.info/. It's well worth reading the information contained in it before you go as you'll get a lot more out of your visit. There are links to other sites from there as well.

One of the main streets in Oradour

Suggested Places to Stay...

HOTELS

Hotel Le Lion D'Or
8, rue du Marché, 86300 Chauvigny
Tel: +33 (0)5 49 46 30 28
Fax: +33 (0)5 49 47 74 28
GPS: **N46.56894 E0.64609**

Notes : 26 Rooms from €47. Open 15th January until 24th December. This is a Logis de France Hotel, and conveniently located right in the centre of the new town. Motorbikes can be put in the car park/courtyard at the back which is locked at night (not undercover). To access the courtyard on arrival go past the Hotel (on your right) and take the next right then right again. The restaurant is very acceptable.

Hotel – Restaurant le Chalet Fleuri
31 Avenue Aristide Briand,
86300 Chauvigny
Tel: +33 (0)5 49 46 31 12
Fax: +33 (0)5 49 56 48 31
GPS: **N46.56705 E0.63879**

Notes : Located a few minutes walk from the town centre. 38 Rooms from €38. Open all year. Own private secure car park.

CAMPING

Campsite De la Fontaine
rue de la Fontaine, 86300 Chauvigny
Tel : +33 (0)5 49 46 31 94
GPS: **N46.57092 E0.65330**

Notes: Opening season from 5th April until 5th October inclusive. €11.50 - €15.90 per night. 120 touring pitches, 120 permanent pitches; total area 208 hectares. Directions - take the N151 from Poitiers to Chauvigny. Turn left in the centre of Chauvigny just before the gate. Follow the signs.

B&B

La Veaudepierre
8 rue du Berry, 86300 Chauvigny
Tel: +33 (0)5 49 46 30 81
Fax: +33 (0)5 49 47 64 12
Email: laveaudepierre@club-internet.fr
GPS: **N46.56872 E0.64707**

Notes: Contact M et Mme de Giafferi. A charming 18th century residence with 1 single room, 1 twin room and 3 triple rooms. This property is located in the lower town centre, the second street on the left after the church.

BAGNOLES-DE-L'ORNE

HOTEL

Hôtel - Restaurant le Normandie
2 avenue du Docteur Lemuet, 61140
Bagnoles-de-l'Orne
Tel: +33 (0)2 33 30 71 30
Fax: +33 (0)2 33 30 71 31
Email: hotel-le-normandie@wanadoo.fr
Web: www.hotel-le-normandie.com
GPS: **N48.55687 W0.41233**

Notes: Located in the centre of the town.
22 rooms from €63.
Private garaged parking available.

tournumber:3

Caen – Ancy-le-Franc – Caen

SUMMARY

Duration: 3-4 days

Caen – Ancy-le-Franc (via Fontainebleau): 486km (302 miles)
Time: 7 hrs 20mins (riding)

Ancy-le-Franc – Caen (via Chartres): 482km (299 miles)
Time: 7 hrs 15mins (riding)

TOUR OVERVIEW

This tour commences from the ferry terminal at Caen (Ouistreham) and takes you down to Ancy-le-Franc, a village located in the Yonne département of Burgundy (Bourgogne), some 190km (118 miles) to the south east of Paris. Ancy-le-Franc, or thereabouts, is the suggested place to stay and the base for exploring some of the delights of northern Burgundy.

The D965 near Chablis

The Burgundy region is one of the most prosperous in France, and is renowned for its wines, cuisine (bœuf bourguignon, coq au vin, escargots - snails) and cheeses. Two canals are prominent in the region, the Canal du Nivernais and the Canal de Bourgogne, the latter passing very close to the south of Ancy-le-Franc alongside the River Armançon.

This tour needs at least three days, but preferably more, as there are two full days riding leaving one day for exploring the region. The last time I completed this tour I spent four days in the region, which allowed two full days for exploring. I caught the overnight ferry from Portsmouth to Caen which enabled an early start from the ferry terminal at 06:30 hrs, arriving at the hotel in Ancy-le-Franc at around 16:45 hrs.

The ride down to Ancy-le-Franc is via the delightful town of Fontainebleau and its huge Palace. Two-thirds of the return journey back to Caen though follows a different route, via Chartres. Although this route back is marginally shorter, it's still a long ride to Caen for the late afternoon ferry leaving at 16:30 hrs, so you'll need a very early start from Ancy-le-Franc. If this doesn't appeal there are two alternatives. The first is to return to Caen using the motorways (A6, A135, A13), about 410km (255 miles), which without stopping is just under 5 hours riding.

L'Hostellerie du Centre at Ancy-le-Franc

The second alternative is to stay on the suggested route back but have an overnight stop en route. Chartres is a convenient town for a stopover, in the Centre region (Eure-et-Loir département). It's about 215km (134 miles) from Ancy-le-Franc, and a lovely large market town with a huge Cathedral. A reasonably priced hotel is suggested below.

ROUTE DESCRIPTION – CAEN TO ANCY-LE-FRANC (VIA FONTAINEBLEAU)

Like most of the other tours, the suggested route to and from Ancy-le-Franc avoids, where possible, motorways and dual carriageways, which is the main reason why the ride takes around 7 hours (excluding stops) to get there. The only motorways included are the A13-E5 for just 23.5km (29 miles), and a short stretch on the A6-E15 towards the end of the ride at Auxerre for 11km (6.8 miles).

Once around the Caen ring road and onto the D613 there is a 144km (89 mile) run east along predominately straight roads, passing Lisieux and Evreux, all the way to junction 15 of the A13-E5 motorway. This stretch of road is not perhaps the most inspiring to do, but it is easy to navigate and gets you nicely set up for the more interesting roads ahead. If you feel like a break at Evreux then a good place to stop is the large caféteria close to the huge Carrefour supermarket as you go through the centre. It's at **GPS: N49.01387 E1.17356**. There's a petrol station here as well.

From Junction 15 of the A13 to Paris, ride for 23.5km (29 miles) to Junction 10, where you head out south on the D191 which takes you to the north of Rambouillet. Much of the D191 is quite scenic, particularly towards the end where you join the N10 through the Forêt de Rambouillet. Remain on the N10 dual carriageway through Rambouillet and down to Ablis, taking the N191 out to Étampes. Good progress can be made on

The D905 alongside the Burgundy Canal near Montbard

The D956 near Noyers

the N191, also the D837 and D409 leading to Fontainebleau, as they are all fast roads. The last 22km (13.6 miles) before you reach Fontainebleau, through the Forêt de Fontainebleau, are very picturesque and on a sunny day the ride is superb. There are many places to safely stop and enjoy the surroundings.

If you have the time then it's worth going into Fontainebleau, even if only for a brief stop. The town has one of the largest royal châteaux in the whole of France, now a UNESCO World Heritage Site. Château (or Palace) de Fontainebleau (**GPS:** **N48.40194 E2.69684**), built from the 16th century onwards, is situated roughly in the middle of the large and magnificent forest mentioned earlier. The château was used extensively by French kings and also Napoléon Bonaparte, as it was a particular favourite as a royal hunting lodge. The town itself, which centres around the château, is quite pleasant with a good choice of cafés, bars and restaurants.

From Fontainebleau take the D606 all the way down to the north of Auxerre, 109km (67 miles) to join the A6-E15 motorway. Most of the D606 is an excellent ride along a good road, scenic in places, particularly between Sens and Joigny. Once clear of Fontainebleau and the forest, and after crossing the River Loing, a tributary of the River Seine, the D606 follows the River Yonne to Auxerre, initially along the west bank to Sens, then the east bank for a while before switching back to the west bank at Joigny. The small town of Sens is quiet and picturesque, dominated by the gothic Cathédrale St-Étienne, built in the early part of the 12th century. The town's streets are lovely, with many medieval houses and buildings. The D606 bypasses the town, so follow the signs for the town centre if you wish to take a break here.

Joigny, like Sens, is another small town located on the banks of the River Yonne. Both are situated in the Yonne département of the Burgundy region. There is nothing spectacular about Joigny but it does have some very old houses on the river banks, and the Château des Gondi which overlooks the town. It is also the departure point for canal trips on either the Canal du Nivernais or the Burgundy Canal which meet in the town.

At Auxerre take the A6-E15 at Junction 19 (to Dijon, Lyon) south to Junction 20, to the east of Auxerre. This is a toll motorway (péage) so you need to have some cash ready to pay at the exit. From Junction 20 take the D965 road to Chablis and Tonnerre. This is an excellent 24km (15 miles) stretch of road that leads onto the D905 at Tonnerre, and the final 14km (9 miles) of the ride to Ancy-le-Franc. The D965 and the D905 combined are superb roads for riding a motorbike on, nice surface, fast, and with some long sweeping bends.

WHAT TO DO WHEN YOU GET THERE

There is much to see and do in Northern Burgundy and fortunately most of the roads in this region are very good to ride on. The following are a few suggestions on where to go.

Ancy-le-Franc

In Northern Burgundy there are two of the finest châteaux in France, and if you are staying at the L'Hostellerie du Centre in Ancy-le-Franc then one of these, the Châteaux d'Ancy-le-Franc (**GPS:** N47.77529 E4.16306) is just across the road from the hotel. Built in the 16th century by the Italian architect Sebastiano Serlio, this Renaissance château has a superb inner courtyard and luxurious apartments. On one of my visit a few years ago, the château played host to a televised international European schools rugby union tournament during the day, which was followed by a superb fireworks display late in the evening from the roof of the château.

Abbey de Fontenay

Whether you are interested in Abbeys or not, you will not regret a visit to this one. Founded in the early 12th century, and

Abbey de Fontenay

fully restored to its former glory in the early 1900's, Abbey de Fontenay is an amazing (privately owned) monastic complex located at the top of a pretty wooded valley with a stream that runs through it. Open all year round, there are so many different buildings and gardens to go through, and so much to read about, that if you're not careful you'll end up spending most of the day there. The Abbey is located only 28km (18 miles) SE of Ancy-le-Franc, **GPS: N47.63916 E4.38784**. Take the D905 road out of Ancy-le-Franc heading south to Montbard. Go through the village (staying on the D905) and on entering Marmagne turn left onto the D32 and follow the signs for the Abbey.

If you spend the morning at the Abbey and have lunch there or in Montbard, there is an excellent circular route back to Ancy-le-Franc. Head back to the D905 south and after a short distance, at Fain-lès-Montbard, turn left onto the D19 to Lucenay-le-Duc. Shortly after the village take a left onto the D954 to Baigneux-les-Juifs. From here head up the main D971 to Châtillon-sur-Seine (**GPS : N47.85829 E.4.57223**), some 30km (19 miles) to the north. This stretch offers excellent motorbike riding with good long bends through scenic forests. Châtillon is very picturesque with a number of bridges crossing the River Seine. It's an ideal spot to stop for a drink in one of the riverside cafés, before heading west on the D965 signposted to Laignes, Tanlay and Tonnerre. Just after Laignes turn off left onto the D953 to Nuits. At Nuits turn right onto the D905 and Ancy-le-Franc is 8km (5 miles) up the road. The total circular route covers approximately 122km (76 miles).

Chablis

Chablis is of course famous for its production of dry white wines. The village is located in the valley of the River Serein (**GPS: N47.81508 E3.80072**), and in the surrounding countryside and on the valley's slopes you will see row upon row of vines that produce the chardonnay grape. Chablis is a pretty village but very commercialised, so much so that buying and tasting wines here can be very expensive. A cheaper option is to go to Noyers (21km / 13 miles) to the south east, or Maligny or Pontigny (4km and 8km respectively) to the north. The obvious route to Chablis from Ancy-le-Franc is straight up the D905 to Tonnerre and then west on the D965 (the route down). However, a very much more rewarding ride is to leave Ancy-le-Franc southbound on the D905 to Nuits and turn right here onto the D115 and through the woods of Nuits (Bois de Nuits). This is the start of a cross country route to Chablis along some very good biking roads. The D115 becomes the D415. At Sanvigne turn right to Noyers. Noyers (**GPS: N47.69667 E3.99572**) is a beautiful medieval village, not commercialised, and worth a stop. Leave Noyers on the D49 but then turn immediately right onto the D956 then D91 all the way to Chablis. The distance from Ancy-le-Franc to Chablis along this route is about 45km (28 miles).

A Circular Bike Route

This is a favourite circular route covering some 144km (90 miles) on some excellent roads. The route for the first 45km (28 miles) is as above (see Chablis). At Chablis, come out on the D965 to Auxerre. Just before Auxerre go over the A6-E15 motorway straight onto the N65 leading into Auxerre. Take the D606 road left to Avallon and Chalon-sur-Saône. This road follows the River Yonne and then the River Cure, and is very pretty. After about 30km (19 miles) at Voutenay-sur-Cure turn left onto the D32 to Joux-la-Ville, and from there the D11 east to L'Isle-sur-Serein. Just before this village, at Dissangis, and after you have gone through the d'Hervaux Forest, turn left onto the D86 heading straight up to Noyers through the Champlive Forest and the Frétoy Woods. At

The southern entrance to Noyers

Noyers, turn right onto the D956 to Sanvigne and from there bear left onto the D415 (then D115) to Nuits. At Nuits turn left onto the D905 to Ancy-le-Franc.

ROUTE DESCRIPTION - ANCY-LE-FRANC TO CAEN (VIA CHARTRES)

The first 329km (204 miles) of the ride to the ferry terminal at Caen takes a an alternative route to the route down, going via Chartres instead of Fontainebleau. From Ancy-le-Franc take the D905 to Tonnerre and then the D965 to the A6-E15 motorway just to the east of Auxerre. Join the motorway heading north to Paris, coming off at Junction 17 and taking the A19-E60 motorway (to Orléans). You need to come off the A19 and join the N60 in order to get on the D950 then D927 to Pithiviers and Janville.

Both the D950 and D927 are fast roads through some pleasant countryside. Just after Janville cross over the A10 motorway, and after a short distance take a right onto the N154 to Chartres. Go through Chartres (unless you are opting for an overnight stay here) and out on the D906 to Maintenon, another fast and straight road. The D983 from Maintenon to Nogent-le-Roi followed by the D929 to Dreux are very scenic roads that follow the River Eure.

From Dreux take the D928 to Anet, through the scenic Forêt de Dreux, then up to Pacy-sur-Eure to join the N13 to Evreux. The N13 is the road you travelled down on to Ancy-le-Franc, and from here it's the same route back to Caen, via Lisieux.

Suggested Places to Stay...

ANCY-LE-FRANC

HOTEL
L'Hostellerie du Centre
34 Grande rue, 89160 Ancy-le-Franc
Tel: +33 (0)3 86 75 15 11
Fax: +33 (0)3 86 75 14 13
Email: hostellerieducentre@diaphora.com
Web: http://www.diaphora.com/hostellerieducentre/
GPS: **N47.77555 E4.16348**

Notes: Open March to November. 22 rooms from €44. Good restaurant. Secure private parking in the courtyard to the rear of the Hotel which is locked at night. If you need to leave early in the morning for the return ride to Caen let them know and they will arrange for breakfast and flasks to be left out for you, together with a key to open the courtyard gate.

CAMPING
Campsite Municipal de Montbard 'Les Treilles'
21500 Montbard
Tel: +33 (0)3 80 92 21 60
Fax: +33 (0)3 80 92 21 60
GPS: **N47.6314 E4.33303**

Notes: Open 1st March to 30th October inclusive. 80 touring pitches; total area 2.5 hectares. Located approx. 22km (14 miles) SE of Ancy-le-Franc along the D905.

B&B
Le Clos des Feuillantines
60 Grande rue , 89160
Argenteuil-sur-Armancon
Tel: +33 (0)3 86 75 04 84
Email: contact@leclosdesfeuillantines.com
Web: http://www.leclosdesfeuillantines.com
GPS: **N47.75650 E4.10863**

Notes: Contact Nathalie and Fabien Boucheron. Located 4km SW of Ancy-le-Franc in the main street through the village of Argenteuil-sur-Armancon. A farmhouse offering B&B, also a Gite, all renovated to a high standard in pleasant surroundings. 5 rooms from €50. 3 doubles and 2 doubles both with 2 single beds. All rooms with en-suite facilities.

CHARTRES

HOTEL
Kyriad Chartres Hotel
Angle Avenue Gustave Eiffel et Avenue Victor Hugo, 28000 Chartres
Tel: +33 (0)2 37 25 97 97
Fax: +33 (0)2 37 91 01 14
Email: chartres@kyriad.fr
Web: http://kyriad.com/hotel/en/FRA22855.htm
GPS: **N48.44623 E1.53766**

Notes: Located just off the D24 to the east of the town near junction 2 of the A11-E50 motorway. 77 rooms from €65. Private parking. Restaurant and Bar. Complimentary internet access.

tournumber:4

Cherbourg – St-Pol-de-Léon – Cherbourg

SUMMARY

Duration: 3 days minimum

Cherbourg – St-Pol-de-Léon: 325km (202 miles)
Time: 4 hrs (riding)
St-Pol-de-Léon – Cherbourg: 328km (203 miles)
Time: 4 hrs (riding)

TOUR OVERVIEW

This is the second of three tours to Brittany (Bretagne), and takes you from the ferry terminal at Cherbourg to St-Pol-de-Léon in the northern département of Finistère. Like the first tour to Brittany (Tour 1 to Dinan) the aim of this tour is to visit a number of delightful places in the area from your base accommodation in or around St-Pol, and enjoy some of the best biking roads in the region.

The 325km (202 miles) to St-Pol is quite easily done in a day because after the Cherbourg to Avranches section the rest is all on a very direct dual carriageway. Riding on long stretches of dual carriageways and/or motorways is something that I normally avoid as much as possible, but sometimes there are exceptions, and this is one of them because it serves a purpose, particularly if you only have 3-4 days available. It enables you to get to St-Pol comfortably in a day and thus gives you more time to explore all that the region has to offer, plus additional time to spend on several exceptional rural roads that are a dream to ride on.

You could of course use this tour as an extension to the one to Dinan (Tour 1). The

Near Perros-Guirec

View from Trégastel

route to St-Pol passes just to the north of Dinan along the N176, so turning off and spending a day or so there before going to St-Pol is an option if you have the time.

If you can, aim to arrive at Cherbourg from either Poole or Portsmouth (Brittany Ferries only) either late morning or early afternoon. The best option is the fast service from Poole (May – Sept.) at 07:30hrs arriving 10:45hrs local time, or the Portsmouth fast service that gets in at 12:00hrs. The normal morning service from Poole (3 days per week) is still a possibility though, leaving at 09:00hrs arriving 14:45hrs, so even with a few stops you should get to St-Pol by around 20:00hrs. Another possibility is to go overnight from Poole.

The final option is with Brittany Ferries on their Plymouth to Roscoff route, particularly if you want to maximise the time you have in Finistère. Roscoff is only a few miles to the north of St-Pol. Most departures during the week are overnight arriving at Roscoff at 08:00hrs.

ROUTE DESCRIPTION

The first section of the route to St-Pol-de-Léon from Cherbourg initially follows the same roads down to Dinan as described in Tour 1, with one exception, don't turn off the N176 for the city but continue onwards. The route description is therefore repeated as far as the Dinan turn off, with the rest of the route to St-Pol added on. Of course, if you opt to stop off at Dinan and stay there before going on to St-Pol, then you should initially follow the route as described in Tour 1, and then revert to this tour for the remaining part.

From the Cherbourg ferry terminal the roads are not particularly spectacular, but it's uncomplicated and gives you a comfortable ride on some good 'D' and 'N' roads. Just over half of the route follows the coastline down the western side of the Cherbourg peninsula to Avranches. Even without Sat/Nav, navigation is easy. Just follow the signs for the towns of Les Pieux, Barneville-Carteret, Lessay, Coutances, Granville and Avranches in that order, and all should be fine!

The route takes you around the town of Coutances, but if you have the time it's well worth diverting off into the centre. On the town's summit is the Cathédrale de Notre-Dame (**GPS:** N49.04773 W1.44483), visible throughout the surrounding countryside, and it is quite spectacular. On leaving the town make sure you come out on the D971 signposted Granville, Avranches.

At Avranches there is no choice other than to join the main N175 dual carriageway heading southbound (Rennes, St-Malo, Le Mont-St-Michel). After about 8km (5 miles) the road leads straight onto the start of the A84 motorway, which you don't want to take. Ensure you stay on the N175 by bearing off to the right where it's signposted St-Malo, Le Mont-St-Michel etc.

Once on the St-Malo, Le Mont-St-Michel, Dinan part of the N175 (becoming the N176) dual carriageway you stay on it for around 77km (48 miles) until it finishes at the junction with the N12 where you bear right to Lamballe, St-Brieuc, Brest etc. You stay on the N12 all the way to Morlaix, another 96km (60 miles), but once you've completed this section that's almost it, apart from a short section of dual carriageway, the D58 (under 10km / 6 miles), heading north to St-Pol.

The N12 stretch takes you past St-Brieuc and Guingamp, but these are both essentially industrial towns and not really worth diverting off to see. Better to keep going to Morlaix, which is definitely worth a stop, or a visit from your base in St-Pol or thereabouts later. There are some notes on Morlaix below, under 'What to do when you get there'.

The return journey to Cherbourg retraces the route you came down on. Just remember you have 328km (203 miles) to ride in order to get on the evening ferry, unless you decide to stop off at Dinan.

WHAT TO DO WHEN YOU GET THERE

The Finistère département hosts many attractions, from its rugged coastline (reminiscent of Cornwall) to the old Breton ports, numerous lighthouses (phares) and enough ancient splendours scattered throughout the region to keep you occupied for months. And, just as importantly, there are half a dozen or so very good roads to ride and have a lot of enjoyment on. Unless you can spend weeks in the area it's impossible to see and do everything, so the following suggestions are an attempt to highlight what I personally consider to be the 'must do's'!

Morlaix

If you didn't stop at Morlaix (**GPS: N48.57785 W3.82801**) on the way to St-Pol then at some point it's worth a visit, if only to ride in and have a morning coffee en route to somewhere else, like the D769 described below. The best way in from St-Pol is to get on the D58 heading south, but come off left after a few miles and onto the D173 as if you were going to Carantec, a small fishing port/resort and actually worth a ride round before continuing on down to Morlaix. The D73 road out takes you straight into the centre. Morlaix is essentially an old Breton port which in the Middle Ages had a thriving trade with England. Part of the old medieval centre of the town still survives, with its timbered houses and cobbled streets, but the overwhelming attraction, no matter where you are in the town and from the roads riding in, is the granite viaduct. This enormous viaduct, built in 1861, dominates the area, carrying the trains from Paris to Brest, the huge port on the far west coast of Finistère and home to the French Atlantic Fleet. The town has the usual abundance of pretty cafés and restaurants, narrow streets, steep alleyways, hundreds of moored yachts, and it's a pleasant place to wander around.

The D769

It's debatable I know, but personally I think the D769 from Morlaix to Carhaix-Plouguer (heading south) is just about the best motorbike road in northern Finistère. It's 39km (24 miles) long (start at **GPS: N48.56389 W3.83935**), initially following the River Queffleuth out of Morlaix, and then through the far western part of the Parc naturel régional d'Armorique. Much of the road passes through woodland and forested areas, and there are lots of lovely sweeping bends, many twisty ones, and some fast straight stretches. Overall, the road surface is good, but not perfect on some of the corners particularly towards the end, so a little care is needed if it's wet. But it's a great road, and when I've travelled along it, remarkably free of traffic. Should you go into Morlaix for a look around then this is a nice add on.

If you feel like a change from the entire D769 on your way back from Carhaix-Plouguer, an alternative is to go on the D769 as far as the crossroads at Berrien, about half-way to Morlaix, and turn off right onto the D42. This too is a very good scenic road, short perhaps, but with some lovely bends. After 10.2km (6.4 miles), and before you get to Coat-ar-Herno, turn off left onto the D54 and shortly after left again and onto the D9 back to Morlaix via Plougonven.

A Circular Tour

This is a varied and fairly short circular tour of some 106km (66 miles), initially through some good countryside to the west of Morlaix, and then to the coastal area to the west of St-Pol-de-Léon including the fishing port of Roscoff to the north. With stops, it's a full day out, and very enjoyable. Come out of St-Pol onto the D58 south, then off right onto the D788 then branch left onto the D69 leading to Landivisiau. At Landivisiau get onto the N12 dual carriageway heading east towards Morlaix. After just 8.2km (5.1 miles) turn off right onto the D118 south. Almost as soon as you get on this road turn off right onto the D712 and ride into St-Thégonnec

The village of St-Thégonnec (**GPS: N48.52073 W3.94451**) is one of three famous parish closes (a walled churchyard with a ceremonial entrance arch) on the route, all very close to one another, and all very pretty. Built around 1610, it is one of the most complete parish closes in Brittany, and the church pulpit, carved in incredible detail in 1683 by two brothers, is a masterpiece.

St-Pol-de-Léon near the hotel

Come out of St-Thégonnec heading due west on the D712 then turn left at Kermat and onto the D31 down to the second of the parish closes at Guimiliau (6.5km / 4.1 miles). Guimiliau (**GPS: N48.48804 W3.99594**) is a very small village with one of the finest calvaires (crucifixion groups) in Brittany. There are over 200 granite figures depicting scenes from the life of Christ. The 16th century church is also worth seeing.

From Guimiliau leave on the D111 west to the last of the three parish closes at Lampaul-Guimiliau, 3.2km (2 miles) away. The parish close of Lampaul-Guimiliau (**GPS: N48.49267 W4.04164**) contains the church, cemetery, a large crucifix (calvary) and a charnel house (ossuary). It also has a vast belfry, built from 1573.

From Lampaul-Guimiliau take the D11 into Landivisiau, then head out west on the D712 to Landerneau / Brest. The D712 follows the picturesque River Élorn along its northern bank, where you shortly arrive at Landerneau (**GPS: N48.45012 W4.25003**), a lively town with plenty of cafés and shops. A good place for lunch!

From Landerneau head north on the D770 to Lesneven and then out on the main D125 to Goulven (**GPS:** N48.62909 W4.29913), then the D70 to St-Pol and Roscoff. It's not part of this tour, but at Goulven you could if you wanted turn off left and onto the D10 which will take you to some of the deep, narrow estuaries in Brittany known as abers. Some of Brittany's most dramatic coastline is located along here, but it's very exposed! The D10 from Goulven to Roscoff is nothing particularly special, but the road is good and passes very close to the sea along the Grève de Goulven to your left for some 8km (5 miles). At St-Pol you need to turn left and onto the D58 which takes you the short distance up to Roscoff.

Roscoff (**GPS:** N48.72366 W3.98187 to Quai d'Auxerre - see later), largely protected by the Île-de-Batz, an island just to the north, is an attractive cross-channel ferry port and resort with ferry links to Cork and Plymouth. The deep water port, opened in 1973, was intended to bolster trade with SW England and Ireland and help boost the local economy, much of it based on fishing. 16th century granite houses are in abundance in the port. Most of the port's activities are along the rue de Plymouth, Quai d'Auxerre, Quai Charles de Gaulle and rue Gambetta (go to the end of the D58 and just turn left). The Île-de-Batz is well worth a visit if the weather is good. It looks closer to Roscoff then it actually is, particularly at low tide, and with its tall lighthouse it's an attractive sight. There are several excellent beaches to go on, especially the Grève Blanche with its white sands. No motorbikes, or cars, are allowed on the island but you can take a bicycle. Access is by ferry from the main pier, and in the summer season they run every 15 minutes.

The Cathédrale of St-Pol-de-Léon

From Roscoff take the D58 out to St-Pol to complete the tour. A quick word here on St-Pol to finish off. The town is well known for two particular reasons. Firstly, it is at the centre of the artichoke growing region and, secondly, for its two religious buildings. At the centre of the town is the 13th century Cathédrale of St-Pol, which dominates the main square. It's really quite impressive. To the south is the Kreisker Chapel with its imposing belfry. Climb to the top of this for fantastic views over the sea and St-Pol itself, weather permitting. If you are staying at the suggested Hôtel du Cheval Blanc ask Madam for a street map of St-Pol and she'll mark a very nice 20 minute walk for you down to the coast where, on a clear day, the views are superb looking out over to the Baie de Morlaix.

Côte de Granit Rose, Perros-Guirec, Lannion

The ride out to this area, located to the north east of Morlaix, is around 130km (81 miles). This is not a circular tour from start to finish because there really isn't a suitable return route that presents itself, so you retrace the route back to St-Pol from Lannion. The coastline around here is broadly known as

Boulders along the Côte de Granit Rose

View over the Baie de Morlaix

the Côte de Granit Rose, especially around the town of Perros-Guirec on the coast, where there are huge granite rocks and boulders, many pink in colour, that have been eroded over time into some amazing shapes.

Leave St-Pol and head down to Morlaix on the D58 dual carriageway. At Morlaix turn left onto the N12 dual carriageway to Guingamp / St-Brieuc. After just 3.2km (2 miles) bear right and then left onto the D786 road to Lannion which passes to the south and east of the Aéroport de Morlaix (Morlaix Airport). The D786 is a good road and is particularly scenic with the sea to your left once you are through the village of Plestin-les-Grèves.

Lannion (**GPS: N48.73115 W3.46017**) is situated in the Cotes-d'Armor département of northern Brittany and is centred around the River Léguer estuary. It is a very lively town and well worth a stop. Much of its recent success is down to its high-tech research in the telecommunications industry, but Lannion is also an historic city with lots of medieval half-timbered housing and old churches set amongst the hills to the east and north. It's a good place for a break as there are numerous cafés, bars and narrow, cobbled streets to explore.

Come out of Lannion and onto the D65 to Trébeurden, through the village and out on the D788 which is the coast road to Trégastel. This is a very pleasant ride and lovely on a good day with the sun out! At Trégastel-Plage (**GPS: N48.83264 W3.51481**) look out for the huge pink granite boulders on the beach. From Trégastel keep on the coastal road for the short ride to Perros-Guirec.

Apart from the numerous pink coloured, eroded granite rocks around the countryside and beaches of Perros-Guirec (**GPS: N48.81549 W3.44505**), the town is a very popular tourist resort both with the French and especially the British. Camp sites and hotels abound, and with its stunning beaches particularly at Trestraou Plage and Trestrignel Plage, it is a very lively place in the summer season. It's a good place to have lunch and relax.

For the return ride back to St-Pol, leave Perros-Guirec on the D788 heading south to Lannion. Go through Lannion and onto the D786 to Morlaix (the road you came in on). At Morlaix take the N12 dual carriageway heading west to Brest, coming off after about 3.2km (2 miles) and bearing right onto the D58 to St-Pol / Roscoff.

Suggested Places to Stay...

HOTEL :

Hôtel du Cheval Blanc
6 rue Au Lin, 29250 St-Pol-de Léon
Tel: +33 (0)2 98 69 01 00
Fax: +33 (0)2 98 69 27 75
Email: contact@chevalblanc.com
Web: www.hotelchevalblanc.com
GPS: **N48.68421 W3.98781**

Notes: Located just off the main square by the Cathédrale. 19 rooms, from €40. Private parking behind the hotel. This is a good hotel for bikers, and not expensive. Very clean hotel and the owners, particularly Madam, speak English. Good breakfasts. No evening meals but several nice restaurants and a very good crêperie just across the road and others nearby.

CAMPING

Camping Ar Kleguer
Plage Sainte Anne, 29250
Saint Pol-de-Leon
Tel: +33 (0)2 98 69 18 81
Email: info@camping-ar-kleguer.com
Web: www.camping-ar-kleguer.com
GPS: **N48.41491 W3.58030**

Notes: Open from Easter to 30th September. 125 touring pitches, total area 4 hectares.

Camping de Trogolot
Grève du Man, 29250 Saint Pol-de-Leon
Tel: +33 (0)2 98 69 06 26
Email: camping-trololot@wanadoo.fr
Web: www.camping-trogolot.com
GPS: **N48.41600 W3.58167**

Notes: Open from 1st May to 30th September. 85 touring pitches.

Yelloh! Village les Mouettes
La Grande Grève, 29660 Carantec
Tel: +33 (0)2 98 67 02 46
Email: info@yellohvillage-les-mouettes.com
Web: www.les-mouettes.com
GPS: **N48.65883 W3.92911**

Notes: Open from 16th May to 6th September. Located about 8km (5 miles) east of St-Pol. 70 touring pitches.

B&B

Les Roses
183 route du Dossen, 29250 Santec
Tel: +33 (0)2 98 29 70 65
Email: mariepierre.rivoallon@wanadoo.fr
Web: http://perso.wanadoo.fr/mariepierre.rivoallon/
GPS: **N48.69010 W4.03276**

Notes: Contact Marie Pierre Rivoallon. Located just over 3km west of St-Pol. Rooms from €41. Typical Breton house with four guest rooms comprising three twin rooms and a family suite of two rooms (one double and one twin). All rooms have private facilities.

Kermenguy
29250 Sibiril
Tel: +33 (0)2 98 29 95 12
or +33 (0)6 61 53 57 16
Email: marieclaude.dimey@wanadoo.fr

Notes: Contact M.Claude and Michel Dimey. Guesthouse offering three double rooms, all with private facilities. Covered parking is available.

tournumber:5

Caen – Auxerre – Grenoble – Villeneuve-Loubet – Castellane – Grenoble – Auxerre – Caen

SUMMARY

Duration: 7 days minimum

Day 1: **Caen – Auxerre** - 368km (228 miles)
Time: 6 hrs 14 mins (riding)

Day 2: **Auxerre – Grenoble** - 378km (235 miles)
Time: 5 hr 40 mins (riding)

Day 3: **Grenoble – Villeneuve-Loubet** - 276km (172 miles)
Time: 5 hrs 14 mins (riding)

Day 4: **Villeneuve-Loubet – Castellane** - 149km (93 miles)
Time: 2 hr 29 mins (riding)
plus the **Gorges du Verdon Tour** – 111km (69 miles)

Day 5: **Castellane – Grenoble** - 204km (127 miles)
Time: 3 hrs 47 mins (riding)

Day 6: **Grenoble – Auxerre** - 381km (237 miles)
Time: 5 hr 41 mins (riding)

Day 7: **Auxerre – Caen** - 376km (234 miles)
Time: 5 hrs 41 mins (riding)

TOUR OVERVIEW

In a nutshell, there are two key objectives of this tour. Firstly, to ride the length of the 'Route Napoléon' from Grenoble to just short of Cannes on the Côte d'Azur in the SE of France, and secondly to ride a circular tour covering both sides of the Gorges du Verdon.

Built in the 1930's to commemorate Napoléon's journey north on his return from exile on the island of Elba in 1815, Route Napoléon is a stunning, and at times challenging route covering some 263km (163 miles). Many bikers rate this as the best motorbike route to ride in France, and it's certainly one of the longest, but there is competition from other routes as well, particularly in the Pyrenées. Nevertheless, it really is one to do, and if the weather is kind to you you'll get some very good photos in addition to having a great ride. Much of the route is on the N85 starting off just south of Grenoble, taking you almost as far as Castellane, around 190km (118 miles) south.

The Gorges du Verdon is located just to the west of Castellane, and the scenery and views on a clear day, in the whole of this area, are dramatic and breathtaking. There is a 21km gorge where the River Verdon has cut through the limestone which results in the largest canyon in Europe, the 'Grand Canyon du Verdon'. The river flows east to west (largely through tunnels underground) before exiting at the Pont du Galetas and filling the massive artificial Lac de Sainte-Croix. This lake on a clear day has an amazingly blue glow to it, and it's possible to swim in it and go sailing.

It's well worth doing a complete circular tour around the Gorges, a distance of some 111km (69 miles), but you must do it from east to west (see under 'Route Description' below for more information). By doing the circular tour you will not miss out on all the views, in particular the vantage point at Balcons de la Mescla in the east on the D71. The road to the north of the Gorges, the D952 (Route des Crêtes), is very dramatic with sheer drops of around 800metres, and for this reason alone you need to take care and keep your eyes firmly on the road. There are a high number of hairpin and hidden bends along here, and unless you have to, try and avoid doing this tour in July and August due to the very high volume of traffic present. The best time to do this tour is in May or September, or early October, and the last time I did it at this time the traffic was extremely light.

In respect of the tour as a whole (from Caen and back again), this is one of the 'big three riding tours' in this book, and in total involves some 2,138 km (1,331 miles) of biking over a minimum 7 day period. This is a lot of riding in a fairly short space of time, on average just over 300km (nearly 200 miles) per day, and in all probability you'll want a few extra days (more if you are able) to relax and possibly explore a little further.

On the N85 'Route Napoléon' near Digne-les-Baines

Personally, the optimum is to spread it out over a week and two weekends giving you 9 days in total i.e. leaving Portsmouth on the overnight ferry on a Friday night going to Caen (giving you a good early start on Saturday to the first overnight stop at Auxerre), and returning the following Sunday Caen – Portsmouth. Your two 'extra' days or more can be spent as you want, but as a suggestion an extra day or two at Villeneuve-Loubet (or thereabouts) gives you

View from the N85 'Route Napoléon'

Lac de Sainte-Croix, Gorges du Verdon

the chance to visit Cannes, Antibes, Nice and/or Monte-Carlo on the Côte d'Azur, all of which are relatively close by. An extra day at Castellane is also an attractive option, particularly if the weather is not good on one of the days for the spectacular trip around the Gorges du Verdon.

One consideration you need to bear in mind for this tour is that for the return journey you will need to get an early start from the hotel at Auxerre (if you are staying there) to reach Caen for the ferry later in the day, unless you are opting for an overnight stay en route at say Chartres (a suitable hotel is suggested at the end). It's a 376km (234 mile) ride back, and the ferry departs at 16:30 hrs.

ROUTE DESCRIPTION

There is some motorway riding on this tour, and in the interests of time and the need to get down to Auxerre and Grenoble in two days to allow more time further south, it really can't be avoided. There is a small section of motorway on the first day on the A6-E15 of some 37km (23 miles) leading into Auxerre (this is a toll motorway – péage), then the longest section of some 205km (128 miles) on the second day from Chalon-sur-Saône down to Grenoble along the A6-E15, followed by the A46, A43-E70, and finally the A48-E711 motorway into Grenoble. After this, you'll be riding on some fantastic and very challenging roads, and the motorways will quickly be forgotten!

DAY 1

This is the ride from Caen to Auxerre, of some 368km (228 miles). Once round the Caen ring road and onto the D613 you have a 117km (73 mile) run east along predominately straight roads, passing Lisieux and Evreux, all the way to the turn off right at Pacy-sur-Eure. This stretch of road is not perhaps the most inspiring to do, but it is easy to navigate and gets you nicely set up for the more interesting roads ahead.

Turning off right from the N13 at Pacy-sur-Eure onto the D836 leading to Dreux, finally puts you on a very scenic road that, for the most part, follows the River Eure. This 29km (18 mile) ride from Pacy-sur-Eure to Dreux needs careful navigation if you are without Sat/Nav, but it's a lovely ride with the final 10km (6 miles) through the Dreux Forest (Forêt de Dreux). And once around Dreux the scenic roads continue for another 20km (13 miles) along the River Eure to Nugent-le-Roi and Maintenon.

From Chartres the N154 down to junction 12 of the A10 motorway is fast and straight. The A10 is avoided, as is the new A19 a little to the south, in favour of the more interesting cross country route on the D927 and D950 to Pithiviers and St-Maurice-sur-Fessard, just before you join the N60 dual carriageway leading to the A6-E15 motorway. You come off the A6-E15 at junction 19 (to the north of Auxerre) and if you are staying at the Hôtel Kyriad Auxerre it's only about 1.6km (1 mile) away.

DAY 2

The second day is spent riding down to Grenoble, a journey of some 378km (235 miles). The first 160km (100 miles) or so is the interesting part of the route, the rest is unfortunately all motorways. The D606 out of Auxerre is a good scenic road which follows the Rivers Yonne and then Cure almost to Avallon, 45km (28 miles) to the south. From Avallon the D606 to Saulieu is fast, and for the most part straight, taking you through the woods and forests of the region. The D980 out of Saulieu to Autun, through the Morvan Hills, is preferred to the D15 as it's a more enjoyable ride.

At Autun you will have travelled about 112km (70 miles), and the city is worth a stop as you go through the centre (**GPS: N46.95002 E4.29896**) to get out east and onto the N80. The city, surrounded by medieval walls, is however very Roman, having been founded by the Emperor Augustus around 10 BC. Evidence of the Romans is widespread, from the remains of what was the largest Roman theatre in Gaul to the two surviving Roman gates. The River Arroux runs across the northern part of the city, which you actually cross as you enter the city from Saulieu.

Keeping on the N80 out of Autun slightly prolongs the inevitable motorway section, but in any event it is a much prettier route to start with than the more direct D978 road to Chalon-sur-Saône.

On the D952 near La Palud-sur-Verdon

At Chalon-sur-Saône you will have completed about 168km (105 miles), about half way to Grenoble. If you are staying in the suggested hotel in Grenoble, La Clé des Champs, then you have about 130 miles to go, which is just over 2 hours riding as it's all on motorways. Therefore, a stop for a good lunch and rest at Chalon-sur-Saône is ideal.

Chalon is located largely to the west of the meandering River Saône, and is essentially an industrial centre, so there is nothing too exciting here. If you stop off here then head for the old riverside area on the west bank of the Saône, you'll find dozens of cafés and bars to eat in. You are particularly spoilt for choice on Ille Saint-Laurent, a tiny island in the middle of the river, off the Quai Des Messageries (**GPS:** **N46.77970 E4.86072**).

From Chalon it's straight out onto the motorways to Grenoble via Lyon, firstly the A6-E15, then A46, A43-E70, and finally the A48-E711. A number of service areas are located on the route, so there are no problems in getting fuel.

Grenoble is a lively city situated on the Rivers Drac and Isère, and surrounded by mountains. If you decide to stay here for a day or two there is a lot to do. If the weather is good, then take the cable car up to Fort de la Bastille which is situated on the steep slopes above the River Isère. The views from here are superb; looking west are the cliffs of the Vercors massif with the highest peak, Moucherotte at 1,901m dominating the city, and to the east is the Belledonne massif rising to 2,978m.

DAY 3

The third day is essentially riding Route Napoléon, from the start of the N85 just below Grenoble all the way down to Grasse. The final part of the run from Grasse to Cannes (only 12km/8 miles) is not included as you need to head out east from Grasse to Villeneuve-Loubet, and besides it's really not worth bothering about.

Head out of Grenoble on the N85 at the start of the run. The road down to Gap is around 72km (45 miles) and the nearer you get to Gap the better the scenery gets. The road is very well surfaced with some good, long sweeping bends and some tight, slow ones thrown in for good measure! It's very picturesque, even on a dull day, but this section to Gap is not rated with the same enthusiasm as the subsequent sections.

From Gap (**GPS:** **N44.55976 E6.07505**) head out south for Sisteron and Digne-les-Bains along the Durance valley, again on the N85 to the start of the A51 motorway. The N85 ends here temporarily and becomes the D1085 then D4085. At this point you could go on the motorway and come off at junction 21 to rejoin the N85 if you wish, but I prefer the D1085/D4085 which runs parallel to the A51 as there are no problems then stopping for photos etc., and it's a very scenic road with the Lure Mountain range to your right and the River Durance and other mountains to your left. It also gives you an easy opportunity for a break at Sisteron (**GPS:** **N44.19454 E5.94344**), the mountain gateway to Provence on the River Durance, before rejoining the N85.

Re-entering the N85 south of Sisteron takes you to Digne-les-Bains, about 24km (15 miles) west. This stretch of the N85 hugs the northern bank of the River Bléone, nothing special but a pleasant ride nonetheless. The town of Digne-les-Bains (**GPS:** **N44.09319 E6.23538**) is right on the edge of some serious mountains, and worth noting is that to the North and East of the town is the largest geological reserve in Europe, the Réserve Naturelle Géologique de Haute-Provence, with fossils going back some 300 million years.

Half way along, the N84 out of Digne-les-Bains to Castellane becomes the D4085, then the D6085 to Grasse. The road linking Digne to Castellane then Grasse, through the mountains, is one of the best stretches

Tunnel on the D71

of road you could possibly wish to ride your motorbike on. It's about 96km (60 miles) and has everything. You'll run out of superlatives to describe it! The road surface is excellent throughout. There are lots of quick straight sections, every type of bend you could wish for from long, fast sweepers, to medium slow twisty ones, to acute hairpins you'll struggle to exceed 20 mph through. And if all that wasn't enough, the scenery throughout is superb, even stunning in places!

Several cautious notes however on the above. There are a number of long drops (just to help keep you focused on the road), and this stretch is sometimes patrolled by French Police motorcyclists with speed guns because of its popularity with European bikers, so beware. Also, there are several fixed speed cameras around, but not as many as one might expect given the route.

After some very twisty bends, you finally enter Grasse, officially the starting point of the Route Napoléon. With impressive views over the Côte d'Azur, Grasse (**GPS:** 43.66023 E6.92910) is world renowned for the production of perfumes, with dozens of perfumeries in and around the town with showrooms and guided tours.

Out of Grasse you head east on the D2085, which is a pretty road to Villeneuve-Loubet, assuming of course you intend on staying at the Hôtel du Parc as suggested.

DAY 4

If you are not staying in the Côte d'Azur for a day or so then day four of this tour is the ride from Villeneuve-Loubet back to Castellane (**GPS:** 43.84587 E6.51340), about 72km (44 miles) to the north west, and then the circular tour around the Gorges du Verdon, some 111km (69 miles). From Villeneuve-Loubet you retrace the route you came in on, part of Route Napoléon (via Grasse) as far as Castellane, then head out west to the Gorges. Coming up from Grasse, it's very tempting to turn off the D6085 before you get to Castellane and head out west to the Gorges on the D21 then D71, and do the southern side first. However, if you did this you would not be able to complete the tour round because there is one section on the northern side, the D952 (Route des Crêtes), which is one way, and it's westbound only, so you need to start the tour from the northern side and go around anti-clockwise.

(**Tip:** depending upon where you are staying overnight in/around Castellane, you might be able to leave your panniers/ luggage at your accommodation in the morning before you head off on the tour around the Gorges)

From Castellane take the D952 heading out west. This is the start of the circular tour that, without exception, has stunning views, great roads, and amazing scenery most of the way! The road surface overall is good, but it's not a fast road anywhere, and there are hazards. At some points there are sheer drops, particularly on the higher parts where there is nothing to stop you going off over the side, and with campervans around and very acute, steep hairpins and blind bends, this route is not for the faint-hearted or inexperienced rider.

Along the northern side of the gorge, running from Castellane through to Moustiers-Ste-Marie, some 38km (24 miles) although it will seem much further, there are plenty of places to stop off. About half-way along is the tiny village of La Palud-sur-Verdon (**GPS: N43.78039 E6.34271**), a good place to stop for a break and a visit to the local bar/restaurant.

Just before Moustiers-Ste-Marie you'll see a turning left for the D957 which is the start of the route for the southern part of the gorge. However, it's well worth going on a few more kilometres and into Moustiers (**GPS: N43.84258 E6.22104**). The village is very picturesque, and with the backdrop of sheer cliffs behind it and the tremendous number of shops, it's very popular in the summer season.

Retracing your route out of Moustiers and back onto the D952, you will shortly bear right and onto the D957 to take you along the southern part of the gorge. After 6km (3.7 miles) make sure you turn off left and onto the D19 (to Aiguines) then the D71. Before turning off you'll see the huge artificial Lac de Sainte-Croix down to your right which is about 10km long and 3km wide, blue/ turquoise in colour and breathtaking to look at. The lake is the result of a dam being built on the River Verdon in 1975. It's now quite a tourist area, with plenty of beaches, picnic areas and most water sports.

Once on the D19 leading onto the D71, the Corniche Sublime, you shortly come into the village of Aiguines (**GPS: N43.77567 E6.24268**), renowned for its wood-turning. At this point you're about 800m high and it soon rises to more than 900m before dipping back again. About 21km (13 miles) east of Aiguines along the D71 you'll come to a major vantage point, the Balcons de la Mescla, (**GPS: N43.74189 E6.38194**) which is an essential stop to view and fully appreciate the Grand Canyon to the west and the River Verdon to the north.

From Balcons de la Mescla you continue east for 11.5km (7 miles) until you come to the outskirts of the small village of Comps-sur-Artuby. Turn left here heading north along the D955 for 13.6km (8.5 miles) to then turn right and rejoin the D952 (northern route) just after the Pont-de-Soleils. This takes you back to Castellane 10km (6.4 miles away) east, and if you are staying at the suggested Nouvel Hôtel du Commerce it is located just off the main high street, the D4085.

DAY 5, 6 AND 7

Unless you extend your stay at Castellane, day five is spent retracing the rest of the Route Napoléon back to Grenoble, a great opportunity to ride it again but this time south to north. It's just as good! Again, if you don't extend your stay at Grenoble day six is the return to Auxerre, and day seven the return to Caen, following the same routes as you came in on.

Suggested Places to Stay...

AUXERRE

HOTEL
Hôtel Kyriad Auxerre
Route des Bries, RN 6, 89380 Auxerre
Tel: +33 (0)3 86 53 25 34
Fax: +33 (0)3 86 53 05 27
Email: appoigny@kyriad.fr
Web: http://www.kyriad-auxerre-appoigny.fr
GPS: **N47.85327 E3.54172**

Notes: Located about 9 km north of Auxerre, conveniently just off junction 19 of the A6-E15 motorway. 110 rooms from €52. Own car park. No restaurant in the hotel, but there is a very good one just across the car park (1 minute walk). The buffet breakfast is excellent! Park your bike right outside the main entrance overnight and ask the man at reception on the night shift to look after it for you. This is an ideal overnight place to stop, but too far from the centre for a longer stay.

CAMPING
Campsite Municipal d'Auxerre
Route de Vaux, 89000 Auxerre
Tel: +33 (0)3 86 52 11 15
Web: http://www.auxerre.com/vos_demarches_reservation_camping.html
GPS: **N47.78585 E3.58794**

Notes: Open from 15th April to 30th September inclusive. 160 touring pitches; total area 3.5 hectares. Located on the southern edge of Auxerre opposite the stadium – just follow the signs for Camping/Stades.

B&B
Domaine Bon-Boire
19 rue de Vallan, 89290 Auxerre-Vaux
Tel: +33 (0)3 86 53 89 99
Email: ca@dessusbonboire.com
Web: http://www.dessusbonboire.com
GPS: **N47.75647 E3.58854**

Notes: Contact André and Catherine Donat. Open March to December. Located approx. 4km south of Auxerre, it is a working vineyard. 5 bedrooms from €48 – two twins with shower & WC, two triples (double bed and a single bed) and a family room for up to five people. All rooms have shower/WC or bathroom. English is spoken.

GRENOBLE

HOTEL
Hôtel-Restaurant La Clé des Champs
2 rue de L'Europe, 38640 Claix, Grenoble
Tel: +33 (0)4 76 98 84 54
Fax: +33 (0)4 76 98 66 22
Email: contact@hotel-claix.fr
Web: http://www.hotel-claix.fr
GPS: **N45.12018 E5.68917**

Notes: 45 rooms from €62. Own private car park. Ideal for a one night stop off, because of its location to the south of Grenoble, near to the N85 Route Napoléon. Not central enough though to the City if you plan on staying a few days.

Continued…

CAMPING

Camping Caravanning Les 3 Pucelles

58 Rue Des Allobroges, 38180 Seyssins

Tel:	+33 (0)4 76 96 45 73
Email:	francoise.amico@9online.fr
Web:	http://www.camping-trois-pucelles.com
GPS:	N45.16708 E5.69898

Notes: 60 pitches. 15 minutes south from the centre of Grenoble. Easy access via the Lyon motorway heading in the direction of Rocade Sud- Exit 5b Seyssin. Not far from the start of the N85 Route Napoléon.

Campsite Bois-Sigu

315 Le Peuil - Veille route, 38250 Lans-en-Vercors

Tel:	+33 (0)4 76 95 47 02
Fax:	+33 (0)4 76 95 47 02
GPS:	N45.11788 E5.58592

Notes: Located SW of Grenoble on the Grenoble to Villard-de-Lans route. At the roundabout ignore directions to Lans-en-Vercors, and carry on for approximately 1 km signposted Villard. You will then need to turn left, clearly signposted. Open all year round. 60 touring pitches; total area 2 hectares.

VILLENEUVE-LOUBET

HOTEL

Hôtel du Parc

1 Avenue de la Libération, 06270 Villeneuve-Loubet

Tel:	+33 (0)4 93 20 88 13
Web:	http://www.hotelduparc villeneuve.com
GPS:	N43.65739 E7.12193

Notes: Hotel situated in the centre of the village by the bridge, close to the River Loup. 15 rooms from €46 all with a bath or shower. Own private car park. Not the most attractive of hotels to look at, but it's well located and considerably cheaper than most of the hotels on the coast and in the large towns. Rooms are not huge, but comfortable with good bathroom. Acceptable for a few nights.

CAMPING

Parc Saint-James le Sourire

Route de Grasse, 6270 Villeneuve-Loubet

Tel:	+33 (0)4 93 20 96 11
Email:	info@camping-parc saintjames.com
Web:	http://www.camping-parcsaintjames.com/gb/camping-le-sourire/accueil.php
GPS:	N43.39618 E7.06257

Notes: Opening season 15th May to 15th September. 240 touring pitches. Take the Villeneuve Loubet exit from the A8 autoroute and follow signs to Grasse joining the D2085. The site can be found on the left, 2 km from Villeneuve-Loubet.

Camping Caravanning la Vieille Ferme

296 boulevard des Groules, 6270 Villeneuve-Loubet-Plage

Tel:	+33 (0)4 93 33 41 44
Fax:	+33 (0)4 93 33 37 28
Email:	info@vieilleferme.com
Web:	http://www.vieilleferme.com
GPS:	N43.42421 E7.05258

Notes: Located mid-way between Nice and Cannes, 900m from the sea. Open all year round. 122 pitches in 2.8 hectares.

CASTELLANE

HOTEL

Nouvel Hôtel du Commerce

Place de l'Eglise, 4120 Castellane

Tel:	+33 (0)4 92 83 61 00
Fax:	+33 (0)4 92 83 72 82

Email: accueil@hotel-fradet.com
Web: www.hotel-fradet.com
GPS: N43.84639 E6.51378

Notes: Located just of the main D4085 in the centre of Castellane. 34 rooms from €60. Private hotel parking. Free internet access.

Hôtel-Restaurant Ma Petite Auberge
4120 Castellane
Tel: +33 (0)4 92 83 62 06
Fax: +33 (0)4 92 83 72 14
Email: boury.marite@wanadoo.fr
Web: www.mapetiteauberge.com
GPS: N43.84592 E6.51288

Notes: Located in the main high street through Castellane (D4085). 15 rooms from €40. Private car park. Free WIFI.

CAMPING

Kawan Village International
Route Napoléon, 04120 Castellane
Tel: +33 (0)4 92 83 66 67
Email: info@camping-international.fr
Web: under construction
GP: N43.51539 E6.29902

Notes: Open from 31st March to 1st October. 274 pitches in 6 hectares.

Castel Camping le Domaine du Verdon
Domaine du Verdon, 4120 Castellane
Tel: +33 (0)4 92 83 61 29
Email: contact@camp-du-verdon.com
Web: http://www.camp-du-verdon.com
GP: N43.50353 E6.29638

Notes: Open from 15th May to 15th September. 390 pitches. From Castellane, take D952 westwards towards Gorges du Verdon and Moustiers. Site is 1 km on the left. This is a superb location!

B&B

Mas du Verdon
Quartier d'Angles, 4120 Castellane
Tel: + 33 (0)4 92 83 73 20
Email: info@masduverdon.com
Web: http://www.masduverdon.com

Notes: Open April to 15th October. Contact Melanie Jacobs. 18th century Provencal house. 5 rooms available, all suitable for 2 people. All rooms have a bathroom, shower and WC.

Le Gîte de Chasteuil
Hameau de Chasteuil, 4120 Castellane
Tel: + 33 (0)4 92 83 72 45
Email: info@gitedechasteuil.com
Web: www.gitedechasteuil.com
GPS: N43.83662 E6.42097 (approx.)

Notes: Contact Nancy and Pascal Herfield. Old village schoolhouse renovated to provide cosy accommodation. Five comfortable double bedrooms, all with private bathroom and shower. Possibility to add extra bed in some of the rooms at extra cost.

CHARTRES

HOTEL

Kyriad Chartres Hotel
Angle Avenue Gustave Eiffel et Avenue Victor Hugo, 28000 Chartres
Tel: +33 (0)2 37 25 97 97
Fax: +33 (0)2 37 91 01 14
Email: chartres@kyriad.fr
Web: http://kyriad.com/hotel/en/FRA22855.htm
GPS: N48.44623 E1.53766

Notes: Located just off the D24 to the east of the town near junction 2 of the A11-E50 motorway. 77 rooms from €65. Private parking. Restaurant and Bar. Complimentary internet access.

tournumber:6

Caen – Latillé – Les Eyzies – Saumer – Caen

SUMMARY

Duration: 6 days minimum

Day 1: **Caen – Latillé** - 325km (202 miles) / Time: 5 hrs 50 mins (riding)
Day 2: **Latillé – Les Eyzies** - 223km (139 miles) / Time: 4 hr 10 mins (riding)
Day 3: **Les Eyzies** – Touring
Day 4: **Les Eyzies** – Touring
Day 5: **Les Eyzies – Saumur** - 292km (182 miles) / Time: 5 hrs 10 mins (riding)
Day 6: **Saumur – Caen** - 236km (147 miles) / Time: 4 hr 30 mins (riding)

Hostellerie du Passeur, Les Eyzies

TOUR OVERVIEW

This is a tour that journeys down to one of the most visited inland areas of France, the Dordogne, one of five administrative départements in the Aquitaine region located towards the south and west of the country. Realistically, it's a two day ride down there and two days back, with the total duration of the tour a minimum six days, because it really isn't worth going all that way and not spending at least two days exploring and visiting some of the many attractions from your base at Les Eyzies (or nearby). There is so much to see and do!

It is possible to travel to the Dordogne in a day from Caen if you want, but it's a long journey (548km / 341 miles), so an overnight stop at a hotel in Latillé (325km / 202 miles from Caen) is put in to break it up. Assuming you come off the overnight ferry at Caen from Portsmouth early in the morning on your first day, you can easily be at the hotel in Latillé by mid afternoon (or one of the other suggested places to stay in the area). Latillé is a very small, but pretty village just off the N149, about 22km (14 miles) east from the centre of Poitiers, which is in the Poitou-Charentes region of France.

With the hotel at Les Eyzies only some 223km (139 miles) away to the south from Latillé, and the suggested camp sites and B&B's also close by, a leisurely start can be made to Day 2.

Whilst a two day stay at your base accommodation in the Dordogne is suggested, do make it longer if you are able to. Spreading your tour over two weekends, 8-9 days in total, will give you the opportunity to explore the area and do more local riding. There are some great scenic rides to do!

A brief note here on the area. Les Eyzies, or Les Eyzies-de-Tayac-Sireuil to give it its full name, is located in the southern part of the Dordogne département, an area that is known as Périgord Noir (Black Périgord). The central part of the Dordogne is known as Périgord Blanc (White Périgord), and the north as Périgord Vert (Green Périgord). Almost all the touring is done in the Périgord Noir area. Due to the constant medieval conflicts that went on in this region between the English and French, the Périgord Noir area is well known for its bastides (fortified towns). Largely because of the history, climate, lovely valleys and rivers, and the general rural landscape, thousands of British people either live permanently in this area or have second homes here.

The return journey to Caen is the reverse of your journey down, with a suggested stopover at Saumur instead of Latillé, which is around 292km (182 miles) from Les Eyzies. Saumur is a little nearer to Caen and therefore it will save you having to get up at the crack of dawn the following day to catch the late afternoon ferry back to Portsmouth. Even so, you'll still need to get going by about 09:00hrs so as not to rush it.

A quick word here on Saumur. The town is spread out along both banks of the River Loire, about equidistant between Angers and Tours. Apart from its renowned military connections (French Cavalry Academy, now home to the Armoured Corps), Saumur is located in a lovely and picturesque setting on the river, and with its 'white' 14th century château overlooking the town it makes it a very good place to stay. In addition, there are many narrow streets with half timbered houses, numerous cafés and restaurants, antique and gift shops, and the largest military tank collection in Europe.

ROUTE DESCRIPTION

There are deliberately no motorways taken on this route, and few dual carriageways. As a result, it does take longer to get down to the Dordogne but it's worth it. The roads in general are varied and very good, with plenty of opportunities to make fast progress

The High Street (D47), Les Eyzies

if you wish.

DAY 1

This is the ride from Caen to the overnight stop at (or near) Latillé. Coming out of Ouistreham on the D514 towards the Caen ring road is easy, but you need to stay alert (even with Sat/Nav) and make sure you take the correct road around the city and come off at junction 11 for the D562.

As you head south on the D562 you are essentially following the River Orne until just before Condé-sur-Noireau. The road from Thury-Harcourt is particularly attractive as it follows close to the river for about 11km (7 miles). Navigating from Caen until just before Mayenne is easy as you remain on the D562 throughout. If you miss the turning left for the bypass around Flers, as I often seem to do, it doesn't really matter – just head straight through the town following the signs for Domfront and you'll rejoin the D562 the other side. Flers is actually a reasonable place to stop off for a break.

The simple way to navigate through Mayenne (**GPS :** N48.30577 W0.61721) is to follow the signs for Laval (N162). Note that shortly after leaving the town you need to take a left onto the D24. Mayenne, located in the Pays de la Loire region, straddles the River Mayenne which passes through its centre. The town itself is steeped in history. Of particular note is it's medieval castle, recently restored, and the excellent museum there. The surrounding area is also well known for its cider production. There are some pleasant cafés near the river which makes it a good place to have a break.

The D24 is a good, fast, cross country road to Montsurs, Vaiges etc., before you join the D21 / D306 to La Flèche. From La Flèche you come out south on the D308 then D938 to Baugé and Saumur. Shortly after you cross over the A85-E60 motorway you need to take a left onto the D347 which takes you all the way into Saumur and out.

Riding over the River Loire at Saumur (**GPS :** N47.27091 W0.08466) is absolutely lovely on a sunny day (it's a very wide river) and this is the perfect place to stop for lunch at one of the many cafés or restaurants. At this stage you would have completed 236km (147 miles), with only about 88km (55 miles)

La Roque-Gageac, by the River Dordogne

to go to Latillé.

Stay on the D347 out of Saumer, going around Montreuil-Bellay to the south, then all the way south east via Loudin almost to Poitiers. This is a good road but not particularly exciting as it has long fast straight sections, particularly between Loudin and Neuville-de-Poitou where you turn off right and onto the D62 that takes you the final 15km (9.5 miles) into Latillé (**GPS: N46.61944E0.07445** for the suggested Hôtel Le Logis Hosannier).

DAY 2

This is the final stage down to Les Eyzies and the Dordogne, a mere 223km (139 miles). Come out of Latillé on the D62 and then onto the N149 heading into Poitiers. The road branches right and onto the N147, which you stay on all the way around the north and west sides of Poitiers before heading out south east. This is actually the road to Limoges, where you don't want to end up, but coming out this way is simpler to navigate, even with Sat/Nav, than the rigors of going through Poitiers.

After leaving Poitiers come off the N147 turning right onto the D1 down to Gençay, and then onto the D741 which is the road that eventually takes you to Périgueux. About 62km (39 miles) from Poitiers you come to the town of Confolens, and it's well worth a stop here. Confolens (**GPS: N46.01400 E0.67175**) is beautiful with a long, narrow medieval bridge spanning the River Vienne, with very old houses on the hillside overlooking the town. The town is known worldwide for its annual International Folkore Festival held in August, where hundreds of thousands of people descend into the little town.

Come out of Confolens on the D948, a scenic section of road, before turning off right and onto the D29 then D54 leading into Rochechouart (**GPS: N45.82498 E0.82104**) It seems a shame that another excellent stop comes up so soon (25km/15.7 miles) after leaving Confolens, as Rochechouart is definitely worth a pause. This very pretty walled town was the site of a six billion tonne meteorite impact some 240 million years ago, thought to be the largest ever to hit the earth. There is very little evidence of this meteorite now, but some of the stone was used to build a number of the older buildings in the town, including another of Rochechouart's main attractions, the 13th century château on the edge of the town. Since 1832 the château has been the Town Hall (mairie) and also home to the Musée Départemental d'Art Contemporain. Before this, the château had remained in the hands of the de Rochechouart family for 800 years!

Rocamadour, from the viewpoint on the D673

Leave Rochechouart south on the D901 (a very good riding road) to Oradour-sur-Vayres and then Châlus (**GPS: N45.65550 E0.98101**), just 22.5km (14 miles) to the south. And yes, Châlus cannot be denied a pause either! The town is dominated by the ruined Château de Châlus-Chabrol, and it is here during a siege that Richard I (Richard the Lionheart) was killed by a French archer, Pierre Basile, in 1199 during a local rebellion.

From Châlus head south on the N21 all the way to the east side of Périgueux, coming out on the N221 then onto the D710 after crossing over the A89-E70 motorway. After about 13km (8 miles) turn off left onto the D47 to Les Eyzies, 16km (10 miles) down the road. The D47 is a lovely section of road to ride and finish the day off. (**GPS:** **N46.61944 E0.07445** at Les Eyzies for the suggested Hostellerie du Passeur).

DAY 3 & 4

These are spent touring the area and visiting some of the many attractions, see 'What to do when you get there' below. Obviously, if you are able to stay for more than two days then so much the better.

DAY 5

Unless you are able to extend your visit then this is the start of the return journey, which retraces the route down. However, as mentioned in the Tour Overview, instead of returning to Latillé near Poitiers it is suggested that you ride an extra 89km (55 miles) to Saumur on the River Loire. There are two main reasons for this. Firstly, Saumur is nearer to Caen, so instead of having to leave Latillé very early in the morning on the 6th day to ride 325km (202 miles) to the ferry, you'll only have 236km (147 miles) to do. Secondly, Saumur is a lovely town, and if you don't leave Les Eyzies too late you'll have time in the afternoon and evening to appreciate it before you depart in the morning.

DAY 6

The final day and the 236km (147 miles) back to Caen (Ouistreham Ferry Terminal - **GPS:** **N49.28304 W0.24934**). The route is exactly the same as the one you went down on.

WHAT TO DO WHEN YOU GET THERE

Where to start! This area of the Dordogne (Périgord Noir) is the one I've personally visited the most, both by car and on the motorbike, so the following suggestions are based on considerable experience of the region and, to some extent, they are a compromise between the need to go on some of the lovely scenic roads in the area and the need to visit some very historic places. With all of the suggestions, I've tried to provide a route that takes you on the best possible motorbike roads. On occasions it may not be the most direct route!

Les Eyzies

If you have opted to stay in Les Eyzies itself then the two main places to visit are all within walking distance. The village is very small, essentially a long high street, but it is very picturesque with high overhanging cliffs on one side and the River Vézère on the other. The area in and around Les Eyzies is historically very rich, and in the village itself (about half way along and partly built into the cliff face) is the Musée National de Préhistoire. Re-opened recently in a marvellous new state-of-the-art building (the museum used to be in the old castle at Les Eyzies) the exhibition is full of prehistoric remains and artefacts covering palaeolithic life, almost all found in the local area.

If you only visit one of the many caves in this area then make it the Grotte de Font-de-Gaume (**GPS:** **N44.93717 E1.02675**), just 1km out of Les Eyzies along the D47 to Sarlat. It is the only cave in France containing polychrome paintings which is open to the public, much of it not discovered until 1901. The cave goes back to the Stone Age, about 25,000 BC, and contains over 200 paintings and engravings, dominated by vivid friezes of bison, of which a group of five were only recently discovered by accident in 1966. Be aware that the numbers of people allowed into the cave each day is restricted, guided tours only in groups of 20 at a time, so if possible phone them up some weeks in advance and make a booking (Tel: +33 (0)5

53.06.86.00). A small number of tickets are available each day to purchase at the gate, but you might have to queue to get one.

CIRCULAR TOUR NO.1

Les Eyzies - La Roque St-Christophe - St-Léon-sur-Vézère - Montignac - Lascaux II - Sarlat-la-Canéda

(All the circular tours assume a start from the high street in Les Eyzies)

Although this is only a short circular tour covering some 61km (38 miles) from Les Eyzies to Montignac, Sarlat-la-Canéda and back again, there is much to see and do en route. Come out of Les Eyzies initially on the D47 to Sarlat, but on the outskirts of the village turn off left and onto the D706 to Montignac. This road, which goes along the Vézère Valley, is not a fast one, in this case an advantage, because it's a lovely scenic road, very twisty and bumpy in places, with two sections where you need to take care due to the close proximity to the road of overhanging cliffs.

After just 8.3km (5.2 miles), and just before going over the bridge spanning the River Vézère, there is a road to your right (D66) leading a short distance to La Roque St-Christophe (**GPS: N44.98949 E1.07125**). This is the site of a prehistoric settlement and one of the largest of its kind in Europe. The complex is located in limestone cliffs some 80 metres high, and goes on for nearly 1km in length on five different levels. Some reconstruction work has gone on in recent years, and as you ride down the short distance of the D66 you will see winches on your right that indicate how the inhabitants brought up their supplies from the valley floor. There is a wooded car park at the entrance to the complex, quite suitable for motorbikes, and a very good café. Take good care on the approach to the car park due to several blind, narrow bends and very low overhanging cliffs.

From La Roque St-Christophe go back onto the D706 road to Montignac. After approximately 1.7km (1.1 miles) you'll pass the highly recommended camp site of Le Paradis on your right, and after 2.9km (1.8 miles) you'll see a signpost to your right to St-Léon-sur-Vézère (**GPS: N45.01076 E1.08911**). It's worth going into this village even if you don't stop, as you rejoin the D706 when you come out the other side. St-Léon-sur-Vézère is rated one of the most beautiful villages in France, and sits on a sweeping bend of the River Vézère, with a lovely bridge spanning the river and pretty houses. The village only has a couple of cafés, one on the riverbank where you can picnic, and a hotel/restaurant. There is a small camp site right by the bridge on the bank of the river, but facilities are very limited, although the setting is superb. Two buildings worth a quick look at are the 12th century village church and the 16th century Château de Clérans, located alongside the river.

Back on the D706, and on to the very attractive, but small town of Montignac (**GPS: N45.06423 E1.16243**). Like St-Léon, Montignac straddles the River Vézère, but unlike St-Léon it has many shops, cafés, restaurants and hotels, and on Wednesdays and Saturdays a huge market. The River Vézère is very popular with canoeists, and in the holiday season in particular you will see them in abundance. But the reason for so much activity here is largely due to the location of the Lascaux caves. Discovered in 1940 by four young boys, the caves contain amazingly preserved paintings of animals (bison, horses, mammoths etc.) thought to go back some 17,000 years. However, in 2008, British scientists using a new method of dating (U/Th) can now put some of the paintings between 25 and 35,000 years old! The French opened the Grotte de Lascaux to the public in 1948, but had to close it in 1963 because the body heat and breath of over a million visitors was severely

The River Dordogne from the terrace at Domme

deteriorating the paintings. Instead, they built what is known as Lascaux II, which is located 2km south on the D704 road to Sarlat. This is an exact replica of the original caves (about 200m away) and was opened in 1983 after 11 years of work costing over 500 million francs. Lascaux II attracts huge numbers of visitors each year (you wouldn't know you were in a replica cave) and tickets must be bought in advance from the tourist office (**GPS: N45.06407 E1.16369**) in the centre of Montignac during the holiday season. All tours are escorted (small groups) and last about 40 minutes, with commentary in either English or French.

Come out of Montignac on the D704 to Sarlat-la-Canéda, about 21.5km (13.4 miles) due south. Once clear of Montignac the D704 is an excellent biking road, scenic in places, with fast stretches and some long sweeping bends.

On arrival at Sarlat (**GPS: N44.89095 E1.21519**), and assuming you want to look around (this is a 'must'!) one of the issues that immediately arises is where to safely park your bike. The best place I have found over the years is to put it in the large, open air, barrier controlled car park known as the Place de la Grande Rigaudie, which is to the south of the town (approx. **GPS: N44.88813 E1.21746**). Note : market day is on a Saturday and the car park is closed as it's used by market traders. The car park is perfectly situated for the start of a walk through the medieval part of Sarlat, which is just breathtaking! From the car park walk north along rue Tourny and enjoy!

A few brief notes here on Sarlat, which alongside Carcassonne in the south east of France is a real personal favourite! The town is the capital of Périgord Noir, a large part of which is medieval with houses going back to the 14th, 15th and 16th century, and some of the buildings going back considerably further. Much of the old medieval part is now pedestrianised and car-free, and strolling through the cobbled streets (some very narrow) and the many small courtyards, passing numerous cafés, restaurants, shops, and restored buildings is extremely pleasant. This area of France is renowned for its production of foie gras (duck or goose liver), and you'll see it on every restaurant menu in the area, and find it widely sold in many of the regions shops.

From Sarlat, for a very short section, come out on the D704 you entered on, but then turn off left and onto the D6 becoming the D47 back to Les Eyzies. This is a great road to ride on (better even than the D704 from Montignac) and it's very picturesque. Most of the road surface is new, with lots of nice gentle bends and fast straights. The last 9km (5.5 miles) is the best, just before you enter Les Eyzies.

CIRCULAR TOUR NO.2

Les Eyzies – Le Bugue - Limeuil – Beynac-et-Cazenac - La Roque-Gageac -Domme – Castelnaud-la-Chapelle

This is a spectacular tour of approximately 90km (56 miles) that covers some of the main attractions primarily along the River Dordogne. It's not a long distance to ride, but most of the roads pass through and along some amazing scenery and some very picturesque villages, and if you stop off at most of them it's easily a full day out.

Come out of Les Eyzies on the D706, a scenic road following the River Vézère, heading south east, then take first right and first right again on to the D703 which takes you the short distance to Le Bugue (**GPS: N44.91816 E0.92744**). Le Bugue is located in a beautiful setting on the right bank of the Vézère dominating the southern entrance of the Vézère valley. It's a pretty village with lots of 18th century architecture, and is home to the largest private aquarium in Europe.

From Le Bugue continue along the D703 for a very short distance and turn left onto the D31 to Limeuil just 3.3km (2.1 miles) to the south. Although rated one of the 'most beautiful villages in the Dordogne', the real attraction of the village in my opinion is its location. It is where the Rivers Vézère and Dordogne meet (these are both big rivers) and it's very impressive. You can park your bike in the easily accessible, open air car park (**GPS: N44.88269 E0.88929**) which is located on the bank of the River Vézère (just) and sit on one of the many benches (a drink in hand from the café just across the road) and enjoy the view of the rivers and the two honey coloured stone bridges crossing each one.

Leave Limeuil using the bridge across the River Vézère, the D51, down as far as Le Buisson-de-Cadouin, then turn left onto the D703. This road, for the next 27km (17 miles) down to just beyond La Roque Gageac is absolutely idyllic, particularly the stretch between Beynac and La Roque. It's a great road to ride as you follow the River Dordogne eastwards.

Beynac-et-Cazenac (**GPS: N44. 83954 E1.14305**), situated right on the river, is very pretty and the Château de Beynac at the top, one of the finest castles in the Périgord region, is well worth a climb up to, if only for the fantastic views. You can leave your bike in the car park next to the river and climb up the steep steps to the château. Both Beynac and La Roque, further along the road, offer boat trips taking approximately an hour, well worth doing if the weather is good to get some terrific photographs of the river and the villages. Beynac and La Roque are both set right into the cliff face.

La Roque-Gageac (**GPS: N44.82570 E1.18274**), just 4km (2.5 miles) further along, is so attractive that it can become too overcrowded in the holiday season, but understandably so. It's a superb setting, again right on the north bank of the Vézère, and with its dramatic overhanging cliffs and lovely housing it's not surprising that the village is classified as one of the most beautiful in France.

Moving on from La Roque, continue a short way along the D703 before turning right onto the D46. Almost immediately after you cross over the river take a left turn signposted to Domme, and follow the steep, twisty road up to the village. Domme (**GPS: N44.80104 E1.21354)** is a personal favourite and one of the best preserved bastides (fortified towns) in the area. It is a tourist attraction, but the little shops are so attractive, and the three 13th century gateways and the views so impressive that this is a definite 'must' to visit. I prefer to take the bike up through the main street to the top of the village rather than leave it at the bottom. There is plenty of room to park a bike there (**GPS: N44.80318 E1.21428**), and it's often less crowded. Make sure you walk to the end of the terrace at the top with your camera for the stunning views over the River Dordogne and the surrounding countryside below. There is an excellent café to the right here that's worth going into.

When you've finished at Domme find your way out (this can be tricky even with Sat/Nav!) and back to the D46, where you want the D50 then D53 to take you west to Castelnaud-la-Chapelle (**GPS: N44.81376 E1.15133**). Apart from the beautiful village, the main attraction here is the Château de Castelnaud (**GPS: N44.81544 E1.14744**), a medieval fortress overlooking the River Dordogne and directly facing its rival, the Château de Baynac, on the opposite side. The Château is privately owned but open to the public, where there is a very popular museum dedicated to medieval warfare.

A good scenic way back to Les Eyzies is to continue out of Castelnaud heading west along the narrow and twisty D53 for about 8km (5 miles) until you come to the 'T' junction with the D50. Turn right and keep on the D50 until you come to the main D703. Turn right to St-Cyprien, over the River Dordogne, turning left onto the D49 at the end of the village. This road becomes the D35 just before you come into the village of Campagne, where you bear right and go up the D706 (the road you came out on) to Les Eyzies.

Rocamadour

Rocamadour is unmissable! The town (**GPS: N44.80177 E1.62005**), with its small population of some 600 people, is actually the second most visited site by tourists in the whole of France (the most popular site being Le Mont-St-Michel in Brittany). The town's location, in the Lot département, is dramatic and beautiful. It is set half way up a cliff along a canyon above the Alzou stream, and as well as its popularity with tourists, large numbers of religious pilgrims come each year to visit the town's many churches and chapels.

The town is surprisingly small, and essentially there is just a high street running through it (between two fortified stone gateways) with medieval houses each side. Above the main street in the steep hillside are seven churches and you have the choice of walking up the long steps to see them or taking the lift. Dozens of cafés, restaurants, and gift shops etc. cater for the huge number of visitors each year. If possible, avoid going in the holiday season.

Getting to Rocamadour is fairly straightforward from Les Eyzies, and almost all of the roads are great for bikes, if a little challenging at times! It's about 75km (47 miles). Leave Les Eyzies on the D47 to Sarlat, through the town and out on the D704A then D703 then D804 to Souillac (from Sarlat just follow the signs for Souillac). At the end of the D804 in Souillac (**GPS: N44.89420 E1.47947**) turn right at the traffic lights and onto the main D820 south to Cahors. This is an excellent road with some lovely sweeping bends and fast straights! After 14.5km (9 miles) you enter the village of Payrac where you need to take a left and onto the D673 which takes you the remaining 19km (12 miles) to Rocamadour. The D673 is a scenic road but very bumpy in places with numerous twisty bends and some tight hairpins. Unless it has recently been done, the road surface in places is not all you would wish it to be! However, it is spectacular in places, very rocky, and as you are quite high up there are some lovely views, none more so than when you get to within a few km of Rocamadour at the top of the canyon (**GPS: N44.80471 E1.62312**), and you look along and down upon the town nestling in the cliff face.

Other Attractions

There are many other places to visit in the area, and you'll see a lot of them as you travel around, particularly caves (grottes) and museums dedicated to prehistoric activity. If you have the time then a visit to Périgueux and Bergerac are worth while, particularly as the roads to both towns from Les Eyzies are excellent. Périgueux, the capital of the Dordogne département, is about 38km (24 miles) from Les Eyzies and is a busy market town on the River Isle. Bergerac is a modern, mainly commercial town with some medieval houses and very attractive squares in the vieille ville.

Suggested Places to Stay...

LATILLÉ

HOTEL

Hôtel Le Logis Hosannier
21 place Robert Gerbier, 86190 Latillé
Tel: +33 (0)5 49 51 88.75
Fax: +33 (0)5 49 54 81 86
Email: contact@logisdelatille.com
Web: www.logisdelatille.com
GPS: **N46.61944 E0.07445**

Notes: 12 rooms from €53. Very friendly proprietors, and their daughter speaks fluent English. Excellent breakfasts. Undercover, locked parking for motorbikes.

CAMPING

Flower Camping du Lac de Saint Cyr
86130 Saint Cyr
Tel: +33 (0)5 49 62 57 22
Email: contact@parcdesaintcyr.com
Web: www.campinglacdesaintcyr.com
GPS: **N46.71897 E0.45811**

Notes: Open from 1st April to 30th September. 185 touring pitches in 5 hectares.

B&B

La Galerne
22 Chemin de Couture,
86170 Neuville-de-Poitou
Tel: +33 (0)5 49 51 14 07
Fax: +33 (0)5 49 54 47 82
Email: lagalerne@aliceadsl.fr
Web: www.lagalerne.eu
GPS: **N46.69063 E0.27804**

Notes: contact Yvette and Michel Pavy. Contemporary house with 5 guest rooms comprising three double rooms and two double rooms each with extra beds. All rooms have private facilities

La Roseraie
78 Rue Armand Caillard, 86170
Neuville-de-Poitou
Tel: +33 (0)5 49 54 16 72
Email: info@laroseraiefrance.fr
Web: www.laroseraiefrance.fr
GPS: **N46.68705 E0.24478**

Notes: contact Michael and Heather Lavender. Elegant house offering five guest rooms comprising three doubles and two family suites. All rooms have en-suite facilities.

LES EYZIES-DE-TAYAC

HOTELS

Hostellerie du Passeur
Place de la Mairie, 24620
Les Eyzies-de-Tayac
Tel: +33 (0)5 53 06 97 13
Fax: +33 (0)5 53 06 91 63
Email: contact@hostellerie-du-passeur.com
Web: www.hostellerie-du-passeur.com
GPS: **N46.61944 E0.07445**

Notes: 19 rooms from €80. Does not have a private car park as such, but there is plenty of space to put motorbikes in the front of the hotel. Have stayed here several times, once for 6 days, with no problems. Rooms are good, so is the restaurant. Superb location in the centre of Les Eyzies, and right by the River Vézère. English widely spoken by the staff.

Hôtel - Restaurant le Cro-Magnon
54 Avenue de la Préhistoire, 24620
Les Eyzies-de-Tayac
Tel: +33 (0)5 53 06 97 06
Fax: +33 (0)5 53 06 95 45
Email: hotel.cro.magnon.les-eyzies@wanadoo.fr
Web: www.hostellerie-cro-magnon.com
GPS: **N44.93996 E1.00993**

Continued...

Notes: Located at the west end of the village just off the D47. 15 rooms from €80. Own private car park.

Hôtel des Roches
Avenue de la Forge, 24620
Les Eyzies-de-Tayac
Tel: +33 (0)5 53 06 96 59
Fax: +33 (0)5 53 06 95 54
Email: hotel@roches-les-eyzies.com
Web: www.roches-les-eyzies.com
GPS: **N44.93498 E1.01769**

Notes: Located on the D47 at the eastern end of the village. 41 rooms from €65. Own private car park. Good facilities provided.

CAMPING

Camping Le Paradis
24290 St-Léon-sur-Vézère
Tel: +33 (0)5 53 50 72 64
Fax: +33 (0)5 53 50 75 90
Email: le-paradis@perigord.com
Web: www.le-paradis.com
GPS: **N45.00176 E1.07100**

Notes: Opening season 1st April to 19th October. Located on the D706 about 10km (6.2 miles) north of Les Eyzies. This is a 5 star campsite and highly recommended. Run by a Dutch family, the setting on the River Vézère is superb. Facilities are excellent. Most staff are fluent in English.

B&B

Le Menestrel
1 rue de Laugerie, 24620
Les Eyzies-de-Tayac
Tel: +33 (0)5 53 04 58 94
Email: contact@menestrel-perigord.com
Web: www.menestrel-perigord.com
GPS: **N44.94000 E1.00924**

Notes: Open all year. Rooms from €55. Excellent location. Private car park.

SAUMUR

HOTEL

Hôtel Alcyon
2 bis, rue de Rouen, 49400 Saumur
Tel: +33 (0)2 41 67 51 25
Fax: +33 (0)2 41 51 34 85
Email: contact@alcyon-saumur.com
Web: http://www.alcyon-saumur.com
GPS: **N46.61944 E0.07445**

Notes: 17 rooms from €42. Secure and locked garage parking for motorbikes.

CAMPING

Kawan Village Ile d'Offard
Rue de Verden, Ile d'Offard, 49400 Saumur
Tel: +33 (0)2 41 40 30 00
Fax: +33 (0)2 41 67 37 81
Email: iledoffard@cvtloisirs.fr
Web: www.cvtloisirs.com
GPS: **N47.26009 W0.06510**

Notes: located on the Ile d'Offard, an island between both banks of the River Loire. Excellent, central location and well equipped site. Open from 1st March to 15th November. 208 touring pitches.

B&B

Ile du Saule Bed & Breakfast
Ile du Saule, 49400 Saumur
Tel: +33 (0)2 41 51 38 71
Web: www.iledusaule.com
GPS: **N47.26229 W0.06011** (approx.)

Notes: great place to stay, just off the D952 across from Ile d'Offard (it's not an island but a small peninsula off the D952). 3 rooms from €38. Private, safe parking. Owner speaks good English. Telephone only to book. Central location to the town. Look at the web site if you need convincing!

tournumber:7

Caen – Chenonceaux – Caen

SUMMARY

Duration: Minimum 3 days

Caen – Chenonceaux (via Châteaudun): 331km (205 miles)
Time: 5 hrs (riding)
Chenonceaux – Caen (via Vendôme): 303km (189 miles)
Time: 4 hrs 40 mins (riding)

TOUR OVERVIEW

This tour takes you to the Loire Valley, and to the lovely but small village of Chenonceaux, the base for exploring the region. Three days are needed for the tour, two for the journey down and back, and at least one for touring. You could easily spend several weeks in this area and still not get around to visiting all the beautiful sights and scenic roads!

The River Loire is the longest river in France, and stretches for 1,013km (629 miles) from the Cévennes mountains in the Ardèche département in southern France, all the way to St Nazaire in the west where it flows out into the Bay of Biscay and the Atlantic Ocean. The central part of the Loire Valley (Centre region), was designated a World Heritage Site by UNESCO in 2000, and most of the proposed touring is carried out in two of the main départements within this, the Indre-et-Loire and the Loir-et-Cher. These two départements are situated in what is known as the Touraine region, the 'Garden of France'.

The Loire Valley has literally hundreds of chateaux and fine houses, not all on the River Loire, and six of the best chateaux have been grouped together as part of a suggested ride, details later. There are many historic towns along the river to explore too, including Amboise, Tours, Blois, Orléans, Saumur, and Angers.

Hôtel Restaurant La Roseraie, Chenonceaux

The ride down to Chenonceaux, allowing for fuel and break stops, will take around 6-7 hours, particularly if you stop for a while at Châteaudun, 48km (30 miles) to the north west of Orléans. A reasonably early start from Caen is therefore needed, ideal if you come off the overnight ferry from Portsmouth first thing in the morning. The first half of the return journey to Caen follows a different route back, primarily to take in the historic town of Vendôme, 65km (40 miles) due north of Chenonceaux.

The bridge over the River Loire at Amboise (D31)

The D952 Bois to Tours road alongside the River Loire

ROUTE DESCRIPTION - CAEN TO CHENONCEAUX (VIA CHÂTEAUDUN)

This section describes the ride down from the ferry terminal at Caen (Ouistreham) to the touring base of Chenonceaux in the Loire Valley. The route is very much across country, and quite attractive in many places. You leave Ouistreham on the D514 then D515 to join the Caen ring road on the N814, taking care to exit at Junction 16 to get on the D613 to Lisieux and Evreux. Getting on this road can be tricky, even with sat/nav, because of the very close proximity of Junction 31 and the A13-E46 motorway to Paris. Ensure you look at the signs!

After just 9.3km (5.7 miles) come off the D613 turning right onto the D40 which takes you down to St-Pierre-sur-Dives. Take a left then right turn to come out of the village on the D4 to Livarot. Worth noting is that just to the south east of St-Pierre, 4km (2.4 miles) down the D511, is the beautiful Château de Vendeuvre, a Norman country house noted for its interior designs and decorations, and also for its superb gardens.

Once at Livarot turn right and head due south to Vimoutiers, then on the D979 to Gacé before crossing over the A28-E402 motorway and onto the D932 to Moulins-la-Marche and Mortagne-au-Perche. The D938 takes you due south on a very straight and quite pretty road to Bellême. Go through the town (avoiding the ring road) and onto the D955 to Nogent-le-Rotrou, and continue through to Châteaudun, 73km (45 miles) away.

Châteaudun is an attractive town in the Eure-et-Loir département, built on a rocky outcrop above the River Loir, a tributary of the River Sarthe. One of the main attractions is the castle, Château de Châteaudun, built at various stages from the 12th century onwards, but extensively transformed in the 17th century into a comfortable residence. The château, which is open to the public, is particularly well known for its 15th century fresco, a portrayal of the Final Judgement. In the old town there are a number of impressive medieval buildings to see. Go to **GPS:** **N48.07036 E1.33217** for the town centre.

From Châteaudun take the D924 for the 54km (33 mile) ride down to Bois, straddling the River Loire. The pretty town of Bois is included in the Châteaux Tour a little later. From Bois, follow the very scenic D952 along the River Loire for 30km (18.6 miles) to just outside Amboise, where there is a turning left onto the D31 to cross the river and around the east side of the town. Once clear of Amboise you ride through the picturesque Forêt d'Amboise before turning left onto the D40 and the 6km (3.7 mile) ride into Chenonceaux (**GPS:** N47.33211 E1.06658).

WHAT TO DO WHEN YOU GET THERE

The Indre-et-Loire and the Loir-et-Cher départements, roughly located between Orléans (the capital of the Centre region) in the north east and Saumur in the south west, are historically rich in châteaux and palaces, primarily because the area was strongly favoured hundreds of years ago by French royalty and the aristocracy. Whilst in the area you should take the opportunity to visit at least one château whilst you are down there, and as all the prominent châteaux are open to the public, the problem can be trying to decide which one(s) to visit and which to leave out.

The roads in the region are excellent for touring on a motorbike, and there are some lovely scenic routes to ride particularly on the Châteaux Tour below, many of which follow the River Loire and its tributaries.

The following suggested châteaux are personal favourites. There are hundreds of others to choose from if you wish!

Château de Chenonceaux

Château de Chenonceaux (**GPS:** N47.32941 E1.06678 for the car park) is within walking distance of all the suggested accommodation options in Chenonceaux, www.chenonceau.com. If you only have time to view one château whilst in this region then, personally, I believe this is one of the finest examples. Built from around 1513 onwards, initially by Katherine Briçonnet, the château is constructed on the almost still waters of the River Cher. With the formal gardens, surrounding park, and not least of all the remarkable architecture and the arches spanning the river, the setting is absolutely idyllic and hard to beat. Inside the château there is much to see, including dozens of old portraits, other paintings

The D924 near Châteaudun

produced by some of the masters, old tapestries, and a considerable amount of renaissance furniture. The kitchens in the basement are also worth going down to see. To get the best photographs of the exterior of the château on the Cher it's worth walking a little way west along the river, through the formal gardens, and then looking back. There is a particularly good café close to the château in the grounds, and it's very pleasant walking through the trees in the less formal gardens nearby.

The Chateaux Tour

This is a circular tour covering five other excellent châteaux in the region, and assumes a start from the main high street in Chenonceaux, rue de Docteur Bretonneau. The châteaux are, in route order, located at Azay-le-Rideau, Villandry, Blois, Chambord and Cheverny. The tour length is 245km (152 miles) which, given the roads and the built-up areas, is about 4 hours riding without stops. Clearly, there is not enough time to go in and see all the châteaux, perhaps only one or two, but they can all be viewed to some extent from the outside without having to pay an entrance fee (the exception to this is Château Chenonceaux above). Most of the roads on the route are excellent and very scenic, particularly near the River Loire and the forests around Blois, Chambord and Cheverny.

Leave Chenonceaux heading east on the D40 for a short distance before turning right to cross over the River Cher, and then turn right again onto the D976. This takes you to the south of Bléré where you turn off left to join the D31. Immediately after crossing the A85-E604 motorway turn right onto the D58 to Cigogné and Reignac-sur-Indre, where at the crossroads turn right and onto the D17, a very pretty road along the south bank of the River Indre to Montbazon, directly due south of Tours. Continue for another 22km (13.6 miles) on the D17 before arriving at La Chapelle-St-Blaise, turning right to cross over the River Indre to enter Azay-le-Rideau. After the crossing turn right onto the D84 and the château is situated a short distance on the right (**GPS: N47.26095 E0.46906**).

Château de Azay-le-Rideau is located on an island in the middle of the River Indre, and was built at the beginning of the 16th century. It's a picture-postcard early Renaissance château with some lovely corner turrets. The interior is attractive but it doesn't compare to the château at Chenonceaux. The landscaped gardens however are very attractive, as is the village itself, and it's worth spending a short time here.

From Azay-le-Rideau continue on to Villandry, a short distance of just 18km (11 miles). Leave Azay-le-Rideau on the D57 heading east, shortly bearing left onto the D120 following the north bank of the River Indre to Marnay. This is a very pretty and scenic ride. At Marnay bear right onto the D7 and ride the 11.6km (7.2 miles) to the château at Villandry (**GPS: N47.34116 E0.51327**).

The main attraction at Château de Villandry, www.chateauvillandry.com, is its beautiful gardens. Again, this elegant château originates from the early 16th century, but it wasn't until the very early 20th century that the château and its gardens were fully restored to all their glory. If you are keen on gardens then this is a 'must visit'!

The next château is at Blois, and from Villandry that's a lovely ride up through Tours on the D952 for 85km (53 miles) along the north bank of the River Loire. The easiest way to get onto the D952 is to go back a short distance on the D7 and turn right to join the A85-E60 motorway (heading north to Laval), coming off after a very short distance at the next junction (7) just after crossing the Loire. Follow the signs for Tours, which will lead you to the D952

Château de Blois is located right in

Château de Chenonceaux from the River Cher

the centre of the town (**GPS: N47.58595 E1.33145**). Whilst the town is nothing particularly special the same can't be said for the château. Most of this Renaissance château was built between the 13th and 17th centuries and comprises of a number of buildings. At various times it was a royal residence, notably for Louis XII, François I, Henri III, Henri IV and Gaston d'Orléans (brother to King Louis XIII). For over a hundred years the château was completely neglected, until in 1841 it became a National Monument and restoration started under the direction of King Louis-Philippe. One of the most notable architectural features is the spiral staircase in the François I wing. Today this large château is a major tourist attraction, with guided tours lasting from 1-1.5 hours. Full information at the official site, www.chateaudeblois.fr

Blois to Château de Chambord (**GPS: N47.61646 E1.51435**) is a short ride of just 17km (10.5 miles). Leave the centre of Blois and take the D956 dual carriageway leading to Contres and Cheverny. After 1.8km (1.1 miles), having crossed over the Loire, turn off right then left to get on the D33 which takes you straight to Chambord (it's signposted).

Built from 1519 to around 1548, Château de Chambord is huge, and considerably larger than any of the other Renaissance châteaux in the Loire Valley. Yet for all its size, the enormous rooms (over 400), staircases, stables, elaborately decorated roof (over 350 chimneys) and so forth, it was largely impractical to live in for long periods of time. Incredibly, the château was originally built as a mere hunting lodge, and mainly used as such by French royalty for short periods, but otherwise it was largely empty and neglected, and at various times fell into decay. Occasional restoration work went on at various times through the centuries, but it wasn't until the end of World War II that lasting work was undertaken by the state. Viewing the château from a distance is truly awesome, particularly close to the car park looking across the fields and the moat (great place for photos!). It's difficult to get to grips with the sheer scale of the building as you view it. Personally speaking, going around the inside (which can take a long time) is not so inspiring, and rather a disappointment as there is not much in the way of furnishings, just one huge room after another! Around the Château is the Parc de Chambord, essentially a wooded park and game reserve containing large numbers of wild boar and red deer. The Parc is enclosed by a 30km (19 miles) wall. For more information go to www.chambord.org but turn your computers' volume control down!

Around 19km (12 miles) to the south east of Chambord is the Château de Cheverny, the last of the châteaux on this tour. Getting to Cheverny is a lovely ride on the D112 through the Parc de Chambord and the Forêt de Boulogne to the village of Bracieux, where you turn right onto the D102 which takes you straight to Cheverny. The château is at **GPS: N47.49939 E1.45989**.

Château de Cheverny was built by Philippe Hurault in the early part of the 17th century, and to this day remains in the same immaculate state as when it was built. Although the Château and grounds are open to the public, it is in fact privately owned by the descendants of the first owners. Apart from the attraction of being able to view a château that has remained completely unchanged on the outside for nearly 400 years, it is the interior decorations, furniture, paintings, and tapestries etc. that are also worth going to see. More information at www.chateau-cheverny.com.

The ride back to Chenonceaux is about 41km (25 miles) and very straightforward. Take the D102 out of Cheverny down to Contres, through the village and out west on the D30 to Pontlevoy where you turn left and onto the D764 to Montrichard. At Montrichard turn right onto the D176 which becomes the D40 into Chenonceaux.

Château du Clos Lucé

A visit to this château, located in Amboise (**GPS: N47.40901 E0.99340**), is another personal favourite, and from Chenonceaux it's a very short ride of just 13.5km (8.3 miles). Leave Chenonceaux on the D40 heading towards Tours, and after 1.4km (0.8 miles) bear right and onto the D81 to Amboise. The last half of the D81 is a very pleasant ride through the Forêt d'Amboise. Note: at the junction with the D31 there is a sign for Le Parc des Mini-Châteaux (**GPS: N47.39146 E1.00555** approx.). This park displays over 40 scale models of some of the more famous Loire châteaux, together with miniature scale model railways and boats. More at www.mini-chateaux.com. At the junction turn right onto the D31 and at the next major roundabout turn left onto the D61 heading into Amboise. After 1.9km (1.1 miles) turn right into rue du Clos Lucé, and the château is 270 metres up the road on the left. The main car park is at the bottom of the hill, but I prefer to park on the verge almost outside the entrance to the château.

The attraction of Château du Clos Lucé is not so much the place itself but the connection it has with Leonardo da Vinci, who spent the last three years of his life here at the invitation of King François I of France. Leonardo, who was born in Italy in 1452 and died at Clos Lucé in May 1519, was a genius with an extraordinary range of talents. He was an inventor, painter, mathematician, scientist, and engineer, to name but a few. He's probably better known though as a painter, his two most famous pieces being the Mona Lisa and The Last Supper. A visit to Clos Lucé gives you the opportunity to go around the inside of his château, to see his study, kitchen and bedroom etc., and also to go around a marvellous display of 40 of his inventions which have been produced to scale by IBM. These inventions correspond to five areas of his expertise, namely Military Engineering, Town Planning,

Château de Chambord

Mechanics, Flying Machines and Hydraulics. There is much more in the museum to see including animated models and interactive terminals that illustrate his work. A visit here is highly recommended! See www.closluce.com for more information. Leonardo was buried close by in the Chapel of Saint-Hubert, adjoining Château d'Amboise (**GPS: N47.41300 E0.98589**).

A Circular Tour

The tour is only some 92km (57 miles), but if the weather is good and you have a 3-4 hours spare then it's a lovely ride, and only two châteaux are briefly mentioned on the entire route! To summarise, the ride starts at Chenonceaux and goes east to Montrichard, then south to Montrésor and Loches, and from there out west along the River Indrois to Cormery, then finally north to Bléré and east back to Chenonceaux.

Leave Chenonceaux on the D40 east to Montrichard, a small pretty town on the River Cher, then out due south initially on the D764 to Loches before turning off left (immediately after going over the A85 motorway) onto the D127/D281 to Céré and then the D81 to Obigny. The D81 is a good, fairly straight road through some lovely countryside, as is the D11 that you come out of Obigny on, which follows the east bank of the small River Olivet down to Montrésor.

Montrésor is a fine village on the River Indrois with an 11th century château that was converted later into a residential mansion. The château is at the centre of the village (**GPS: N47.15633 E1.20167**), with many small pretty houses set along the river, some of which are medieval and half-timbered.

Leave Montrésor heading south on the D760, through the attractive Forêt de Loches, all the way into Loches itself, about 16km (10 miles) away. If you intent stopping off here for a break then head for the old medieval part of the town. The Hôtel de Ville is fairly central (**GPS: N47.12834 E0.99752**) and easy to find as you come in over the River Indre (don't take the right turn along the river, just continue straight ahead). The old town has quite a few medieval monuments, and the town itself is surrounded by ramparts. And yes, there is a Château de Loches, a former military fortress set high above the River Indre, which is very large and tends to dominate the old town. It's more famed now for its massive keep. Former owners and residents of the château include Henry II of England and his son, Richard the Lionheart (Richard I).

Come out of Loches on the D764 then turn left onto the D31, to Bléré and Amboise. After 7km (4.3 miles), at St-Quentin-sur-Indrois, turn left onto the D10 down to Azay-sur-Indre where you turn right onto the D17 all the way to Cormery. The D10 follows the valley of the River Indrois, where the lovely surrounding countryside is very picturesque, as is the D17 to Cormery which follows the larger River Indre, through several very attractive small villages. The distance from St-Quentin to Cormery is 18.5km (11.5 miles).

At Cormery turn right onto the D943 for a very short distance, before turning right onto the D45 and then D976 to Bléré. At Bléré you can either stay on the D976 to get back the 10km (6.2 miles) to Chenonceaux, or go through Bléré and take a right onto the D40.

Other Places

As you will have gathered, there are many other châteaux in the area to visit. There are also a number of interesting towns worth a visit if time allows. The town of Tours is the closest to Chenonceaux (30km/18 miles) and the largest town in the Indre-et-Loire département. It's a thriving place, and if you decide to go then head for the old town and Place Plumereau (**GPS : N47.39442 E0.68145**). Further along the Loire to the west there is Saumur (96km/60 miles) and then Angers (146km/90 miles), both worth a ride out to. Going east from Chenonceaux along the Loire the other main town apart from Blois is the capital of the Centre region, Orléans, about 103km (64 miles) away.

ROUTE DESCRIPTION - CHENONCEAUX TO CAEN (VIA VENDÔME)

As mentioned earlier, the first half of the route back to the Caen ferry at Ouistreham from Chenonceaux is different to the one you came down on, as it goes through the pretty town of Vendôme instead of Châteaudun.

Leave Chenonceaux on the D40 heading towards Tours, and after 1.4km (0.8 miles) bear right and onto the D81 to Amboise. At the junction with the D31 turn right and stay on the D31 past Amboise and over the River Loire all the way up to Château-Renault, where you go around the town on the N10 heading north east and up to Vendôme. Located in the Centre region, in the Loir-et-Cher département, Vendôme is the regions capital and a good place to break your journey. The town is split by the River Loir which creates some lovely views. It was extensively damaged during the Second World War but has been largely rebuilt. South of the town are the ruins of the 11th century castle of the Counts of Vendôme.

From Vendôme take the D957 to Épuisay, turning left onto the D357 to St-Calais for 13km (8 miles). At St-Calais turn right onto the rather straight D1 heading north through Vibraye to La Ferté-Bernard, 31km (19 miles) away. The D1 just before and after Vibraye is quite scenic, particularly the section through the Forêt de Vibraye. From La Ferté head north-east on the D323 to Nogent-le-Rotrou, turning off after 8.7km (5.4 miles) onto the D107 to St-Germain-de-la-Coudre. In the village turn right onto the D7 all the way to Bellême. The rest of the journey from Bellême to Caen is the same as the route down.

Suggested Places to Stay...

HOTELS

Hôtel Restaurant La Roseraie

7 rue de Docteur Bretonneau,
37150 Chenonceaux

Tel :	+33 (0)2 47 23 90 09
Fax :	+33 (0)2 47 23 91 59
Email :	sfiorito@wanadoo.fr
Web :	http://www.hotel-chenonceau.com
GPS :	N47.33210 E1.06659

Notes: Located in the main high street at Chenonceaux (on the D40). Stayed here many times. Highly recommend, they don't come any better. Owned by Sophie and Laurent, both of whom speak excellent English. Laurent is a biker (got a BMW but doesn't have the time to use it much). Private secure parking locked at night – bike can go undercover. Very good rooms. Small swimming pool, nice bar, and very good breakfasts. 18 Rooms, from €53. Château de Chenonceaux is a 3 minute walk away.

Hôtel Restaurant Le Relais

10 rue de Docteur Bretonneau,
37150 Chenonceaux

Tel:	+33 (0)2 47 23 98 11
Fax:	+33 (0)2 47 23 84 07
Email:	info@chenonceaux.com
Web:	http://www.chenonceaux.com/uk
GPS:	N47.33195 E1.06679

Notes: Located in the main high street at Chenonceaux (on the D40), almost opposite the Hôtel Restaurant La Roseraie. Stayed here several times and it's most acceptable. English is well spoken by several of the staff. Bike can either be left on the front courtyard or in a locked garage at night. Good restaurant. 24 Rooms, from €50.

CAMPING

Campsite le Moulin Fort

37150 Francuil-Chenonceaux
(just off the D80)

Tel:	+33 (0)2 47 23 86 22
Fax:	+33 (0)2 47 23 80 93
Email:	lemoulinfort@wanadoo.fr
Web:	http://www.lemoulinfort@wanadoo.fr
GPS:	N47.32693 E1.08577

Notes: Opening season from 1st April to 30th September inclusive. 137 touring pitches; total area 3 hectares. Château Chenonceaux is approximately 1 km away. This is a British owned camp site, very friendly and accommodating. Stayed here several times, and it is an excellent place to camp, right alongside the River Cher, with good facilities.

B&B

Le Clos Mony

6 rue des Bleuets, 37150 Chenonceaux

Tel:	+33 (0)2 47 23 82 68
Email:	clos.mony@wanadoo.fr
Web:	www.france-bonjour.com/clos-mony
GPS:	N47.33309 E1.06962

Notes: Contact is Betty le Clainche. Open all year. Rooms from €49. 19th century farmhouse offering three rooms, with an additional two rooms available in a house opposite the farmyard. All rooms have bathroom or WC and shower. Private parking available.

tournumber:8

Caen – Chenonceaux – Maringues – Meyrueis – Châtelguyon – Chenonceaux – Caen

SUMMARY

Duration: 11 days minimum

Day 1:	**Caen - Chenonceaux** - 306km (190 miles) Time: 4 hrs 32 mins (riding)
Day 2:	**Chenonceaux - Maringues** - 308km (191 miles) Time: 4 hr 52 mins (riding)
Day 3:	**Maringues - Meyrueis** - 311km (193 miles) Time: 5 hrs 6 mins (riding)
Day 4-7:	**Meyrueis** - Touring
Day 8:	**Meyrueis - Châtelguyon** - 331km (205 miles) Time: 5 hrs 19 mins (riding)
Day 9:	**Châtelguyon** – Touring
Day 10:	**Châtelguyon – Chenonceaux** – 281km (175 miles) Time: 4 hrs 26 mins (riding)
Day 11:	**Chenonceaux – Caen** - 303km (189 miles) Time: 4 hrs 24 mins (riding)

TOUR OVERVIEW

Similar in many ways to the Pyrenees tour (Tour 10), this one offers some of the most spectacular and challenging riding you can do in southern France. From your base accommodation in or around Meyrueis in the Parc National des Cévennes, there is a four day period touring the Gorges du Tarn, the Cévennes mountains and Mont Aigoual, Millau (including the new Grand Viaduct du Millau), the Cirque de Navacelles, and for the more adventurous, a very full day out to the Gorges de l'Ardèche. In addition, on the return journey to Caen through the département of the Massif Central, there is a stop off for a day at Châtelguyon so as to ride up to the top of the Puy de Dôme, an old volcanic plug over 1400 metres high.

If you do all of the suggested touring from Meyrueis then you will definitely need the 11 days. This can be reduced to 10 days if you decide not to ride out to the Gorges de l'Ardèche, which is a long ride out and back from Meyrueis, some 372km (231 miles) of spectacular riding, but for the most part along slow twisty roads with multiple hairpin bends, and therefore the 372km will seem considerably longer! (Note: the Gorges de l'Ardèche, Avignon and other areas in Provence and the Côte d'Azur are part of another tour to be published in Edition 2).

Apart from the suggested trip to the Gorges de l'Ardèche, Meyrueis, in the Lozère département of the Languedoc-Roussillon region, is perfectly located for touring the area as it is on the edge of the Cévennes mountains and only some 21km (13 miles) to the east of the southern approach to the Gorges du Tarn. The town of Millau is just another 20km (12 miles) further on to the west from here, with the new Grand Viaduct du Millau just the other side. Opened in 2004 to relieve the horrendous bottle neck in the town during the holiday season for people

River Tarn in the Gorges du Tarn

travelling to and from the Côte d'Azur, this new bridge has also become quite a tourist attraction. One of the tours suggested below takes you across it.

The two stop overs on the way down at Chenonceaux and then Maringues both involve riding just under 320km (200 miles) each day, which is a good distance to cover particularly as the routes are across country. Chenonceaux, which is also the base location for Tour 7 covering the Loire Valley and the main Châteaux, is a pretty village on the northern bank of the River Cher, where the famous Château de Chenonceaux straddles the river. Maringues, just to the east of Clermont-Ferrand in the Massif Central, is by comparison a very ordinary French village with no claims to fame whatsoever! However, the suggested hotel on the southern outskirts of this village, the excellent Le Clos Fleuri, is perfectly located to commence the ride down along the fantastic D906 the following day to Meyrueis.

Overall, this tour involves over 2,300km (1,429 miles) of riding which does not include the ride to the Gorges de l'Ardèche should you opt to do it. The roads used in the four days of touring from the base at Meyrueis are an absolute delight, and some of the most scenic anywhere in France, particularly through the forests in the Cévennes which are stunning on a good day. But you need to be aware that for the most part the roads are very challenging in places; there are numerous tight ascending and descending hairpin bends, narrow in places, often at altitude particularly in the Cévennes Mountains, with the added complication at times of other road users. If you can, avoid going here in July and August.

ROUTE DESCRIPTION

Apart from a very small 20km (12.4 miles) section on the A71-E11 in the Massif Central travelling south, and a short section of 38km (23 miles) on the A89-E70 / A710 on the return journey, there are no other motorways used riding down from Caen to Meyrueis and back.

DAY 1

This is the ride down from the ferry terminal at Caen (Ouistreham) to the first overnight stop at Chenonceaux in the Loire Valley. The first half of the route down, as far as Bellême, is the same as the ride down in Tour 7, thereafter it's unique to this tour. The route is very much across country, quite attractive in places, but not in the same league as the roads in the Cévennes and other areas to the south you'll cover later. You leave Ouistreham on the D514 then D515 to join the Caen ring road on the N814, taking care to exit at Junction 16 to get on the D613 to Lisieux and Evreux. Getting on this road can be tricky, even with sat/nav, because of the very close proximity of Junction 31 and the A13-E46 motorway to Paris. Ensure you look at the signs!

After just 9.3km (5.7 miles) come off the D613 turning right onto the D40 down to St-Pierre-sur-Dives, where you take a left then a right turn to come out of the village on the D4 to Livarot. Worth noting is that just to the south east of St-Pierre, 4km (2.4 miles)

La Melène on the D907 Gorges du Tarn

down the D511, is the beautiful Château de Vendeuvre, a Norman country house noted for its interior designs and decorations, also for its gardens.

Once at Livarot turn right and head due south to Vimoutiers then out on the D979 to Gacé before crossing over the A28-E402 motorway and onto the D932 to Moulins-la-Marche and Mortagne-au-Perche. The D938 takes you due south on a very straight and quite pretty road down to Bellême where you need to come out on the D7, but only for 10km (6.2 miles) before turning left at St-Germain-de-la-Coudre onto the D107 to Le Theil. The reason for coming off the D7 at this point is because navigating through La Ferté-Bernard further south to get onto the D1 is very difficult, so going across to Le Theil and then down on the D323 to the D1 at La Ferté is much simpler.

The D1 through Vibraye to St-Calais is a good road, straight but quite scenic, particularly the section through the Forêt de Vibraye. At St-Calais turn left onto the D357 for 13km (8 miles) before turning right onto the D957 to the historical town of Vendôme. Located in the Centre region, in the Loir-et-Cher département, Vendôme is the regions capital and a good place to take a break. The town is split by the River Loir and is quite pretty. It was extensively damaged during the Second World War but has largely been rebuilt. South of the town are the ruins of the 11th century castle of the Counts of Vendôme.

Come out of Vendôme on the N10 heading south east to Château-Renault, staying on the N10 around the east of the town and heading south to cross over the A10-E5-E60 motorway to the D31 leading down to the River Loire. Cross the river at Amboise staying on the D31 as far as the River Cher. Turn left onto the D40. Chenonceaux is a short distance along this road.

DAY 2

This second day is the ride down to Meringues in the Massif Central, about 308km (191 miles) to the south east. It's easier to leave Chenonceaux by heading out east through the village and turning immediate right across the River Cher and then right again and onto the D976. This takes you to the south of Bléré where you turn off left to join the D31, a good route down to Loches, particularly the 7km (4.3 miles) through the Forêt de Loches.

From Loches it's out on the D943 all the way to Châteauroux via Châtillon-sur-Indre, a lovely town on the south side of the River Indre. Although Châteauroux is only 107km (66 miles) from Chenonceaux, it's worth a short stop here. The town is the capital of the Indre département in the Centre region and is quite picturesque, particularly where the river winds its way through. Nearby is the Château Raoul, which dates back to the 15th century.

From Châteauroux continue on the D943 through La Châtre to Montluçon, some 96km (60 miles) south east. Montluçon sits right on the River Cher in the Auvergne region (Allier département), and is an attractive town especially around the centre, which is mainly medieval. The old town of Montluçon is dominated by the château on the hill, where you will find 15th and 16th century wooden houses.

Come out of Montluçon on the D2144, the main road heading south east to Châtelguyon (the overnight stop on the way back), Riom and Clermont-Ferrand. Whilst most of the D2144 is rather mundane, it does become more interesting after the village of St-Éloy-les-Mines and further along after crossing over the Gorges de la Sioule and the river further south. The simplest route to Maringues from here is to come off the D2144 and join the A71-E11 motorway at Junction 12.1, and go south for a short distance to come off at Junction 14 and onto the D210 then D224. From this junction the suggested hotel, Le Clos Fleuri, is only 18km (11 miles) away.

DAY 3

Once on the D906, just 17km (10.5 miles)

View from the top of Mont Aigoual

The D986 through the centre of Meyrueis

east of Maringues, the roads all the way down to Meyrueis in the south, about 311km (193 miles), are absolutely brilliant. The D906 is a real favourite and you stay on it for 122km (76 miles) until just before you come into the town of Le Puy-en-Velay. If the weather is good you'll feel like turning back and doing it again! The whole area down to Meyrueis through the Massif Central is very hilly and mountainous, much of it through forests of pine, beech and fir. One of the best early sections is from Pont-de-Dore, 14km / 8.6 miles) south of where you get on the D906, down to the little town of Ambert, long ago the centre of papermaking in France. This 47km (29 mile) ride essentially follows the River Dore, very picturesque and with a lovely section alongside the river with long sweeping bends!

Just before Le Puy-en-Velay, in the Haute-Loire département, join the N102, which will take you into the centre of the town. It's worth a stop at Le Puy, a town listed as a 'Ville d'Art et d'Histoire, and as you approach it you won't be able to miss the huge statue, painted red, of the Virgin Mary and Child overlooking the whole area from the Rocher Corneille. Apart from lentils, Le Puy is also famous for being the start of the 1,600 km path to Santiago de Compostella which many pilgrims follow. One of the main attractions in the town though is its cathedral, which is listed as a UNESCO World Heritage Site.

From Le Puy take the N88 southbound all the way to Mende. Again, this 86km (53 mile) section is a dream to ride; great mountainous scenery both sides of the road, lots of fast straights, with a good mixture of slow tight bends and long sweepers. Mende is the capital town of the Lozère département located in the upper Lot Valley, at the northern edge of the Parc National des Cévennes. Again, like Le Puy, it's worth a stop here. It's very pretty down by the river, and the town has many narrow streets with attractive medieval buildings, lots of fountains, and not least of all, the 14th century cathedral and 13th century Notre-Dame Bridge.

Leave Mende on the N88 and almost immediately turn off left to join the N106 to Florac. The town is in the Tarnon river valley, sandwiched between the edge of the Causse Méjean to the west and the Bouges Mountains to the east. The headquarters for the Parc National des Cévennes is located here at the Château de Florac, which provides help and information on the area to visitors.

From Florac take the D907 down to the tiny village of Le Mazel before turning right onto the D907 then D996 to Meyrueis. The distance from Florac to Meyrueis is about 33km (20 miles), along a scenic but quite twisty road in places.

DAYS 4, 5, 6, & 7

These are the four touring days from your base accommodation at or near Meyrueis. All of the suggested tours start from the suggested Hôtel Restaurant Le Family in the main high street of Meyrueis, the D986. A brief word here on Meyrueis itself. This small town is situated on the River Jonte and is surrounded by very contrasting landscapes. To the north and west, and the south west are the Causse Méjean and the Causse Noir, limestone plateaux, largely wild and barren, thinly populated and rising to over a 1000m high. To the east and south east are the heavily forested Cévennes Mountains and the Parc National des Cévennes. The town itself is quite attractive, and there is a good choice of restaurants and bars.

Gorges de la Jonte, Gorges du Tarn

From Meyrueis it's better to start the ride into the Tarn Gorges from the south at Le Rozier, which has the added benefit of a lovely ride for 21km (13 miles) on the D996 out of the town. The D996 follows the River Jonte through the Gorges de la Jonte, with the Causse Méjean to your right and the Causse Noir to your left. This is quite a 'wild' road in places due to the rugged high limestone cliffs and rocks above you – look out for the vultures and other birds of prey gliding high above you when you stop to take in the views.

At Le Rozier (**GPS: N44.19066 E3.20771**), a pretty place to stop for a break, turn off right onto the D907 and the start of the Tarn Gorges. The ride along the gorges from Le Rozier in the south to Ispagnac to the north east (almost to the end of the gorges) is about 53km (33 miles). At Ispagnac (**GPS: N44.37075 E3.53525**) there are three ride options for the return journey to Meyrueis. You could complete a circular tour by going down to Florac and then on to Meyrueis (the road you arrived on), or retrace the route back as far as Ste-Énimie and take the D986 road south across the Causse Méjean, or return on the route you came in on.

Riding up the Tarn Gorges, which are some of the deepest gorges to be found anywhere in Europe, is spectacular and very picturesque. The gorges follow the River Tarn between the limestone plateaux of the Causse de Sauveterre and the Causse Méjean. In places it is over 1000m wide and much of the sides and the valley floor are covered with trees until it gets up to the

View from the D996 of the Gorges de la Jonte

limestone plateau at the top. There are a number of small villages on the route offering places to eat and drink. There are also many opportunities to hire canoes on the river.

The road up the gorges is quite narrow and very twisty in places, with numerous blind bends and in places some quite low overhanging rocks. You'll find you will have to concentrate entirely on the road whilst riding and make use of the viewing points when you come to them. It gets extremely busy here in July and August.

There are some lovely views throughout the route. One of the first you come to is near St-Rome-de-Dolan (**GPS:** N44.27447 E3.21616) just to the east of Les Vignes. To see this view you need to turn left off the D907 at Les Vignes and onto the D995 up to St-Rome, a short but very steep road full of continuous hairpin bends, but well worth the effort. Back on the D907 the next best views are found at Cirque des Baumes (**GPS:** N44.30806 E3.24818), where you'll see lovely coloured rocks and trees, and if you're feeling fit, then climb up the footpath to the 'Point Sublime' to get far reaching and stunning views of the gorges.

La Mèlane (**GPS:** N44.30129 E3.32057) is a pretty village, and just a short distance further on is the Cirque de Pougnadoires, an area of misshapen cliffs, caves and rocks. Further on is the picturesque village of Ste-Énimie (**GPS:** N44.36547 E3.41212), a definite stop off with an excellent car park right by the river to put your bike. From here Ispagnac is about 17km (10.5 miles) away.

Millau, Grotte de Dargilan, Aven Armand

This is the ride out to Millau and the Grand Viaduct du Millau, the bridge that carries the A75-E11 motorway across the Tarn Valley. This is followed on the way back by a visit to the wonderful caves at the Grotte de Dargilan and/or the huge cavern at Aven Armand.

For a direct route to Millau from Meyrueis take the D996 out of the town and along the Gorges de la Jonte (description above). At Le Rozier head out west on the D907 becoming the D809 to the northern outskirts of Millau. Don't go into the town from here, but turn right onto the D911 which will take you up to Junction 45 of the A75-E11 motorway. Before this junction look out for a road to your left. Ride down it for about 3km where there is an ideal spot to take photographs of the bridge. Back on the D911 to Junction 45, take the A75 motorway heading south, signposted to Montpellier. There is an 18 lane toll station as you come onto the motorway, where for a motorbike you have to pay around €3.09 to €3.70 depending on the season. The new Grand Viaduct du Millau is about 5km (3.1 miles) south of here.

Opened in December 2004, the Millau Viaduct is a 2.4km (1.5 mile) cable-stayed bridge towering above the Tarn Valley. Designed by the British Architect Norman Foster and the Structural Engineer Michel Virlogeux, the bridge took just over 3 years to complete, and the cost of nearly €400m was entirely privately financed. It is the tallest vehicular bridge in the world, with seven piers/pylons, two of which are the highest in the world at 244.96 metres and 221.05 metres. The central pylon is just taller than the Eiffel Tower. (Note: no stopping is allowed on the bridge).

Come off the motorway at Junction 47 and take the D809 into Millau (**GPS:** N44.09972 E3.07973). The town occupies a beautiful site on a bend of the River Tarn, where it was once a major manufacturer of leather goods, particularly gloves, in France. It is a lovely place to spend some time in, and with its many restaurants, bars and cafés, a good place for lunch.

Head north out of Millau and back out on the D809 then D907 to Le Rozier. From here head back on the D996 along the Gorges de la Jonte to Meyrueis. If you intend going

The new Grand Viaduct du Millau across the Tarn Valley

to the Grotte de Dargilan (**GPS: N44.19594 E3.37804**), which I highly recommend, then you have a choice of two routes. The easier one is to go back into Meyrueis, out along the D986 (past the Hôtel Restaurant Le Family) where at the roundabout 400m along you take a sharp right onto the D39 which takes you up onto the Causse Noir plateau. After 6.3 km (4 miles) turn right onto the D139 and the grotte is at the end of this road. The more challenging and difficult route (at least initially) is to come off the D996 just before Le Maniel (exactly 6.5km / 4 miles from the centre of Le Rozier) and turn right over the bridge heading for Veyreau (road number unknown). At Veyreau turn left onto the D584 and keep going across the barren Causse Noir until you come to the crossroads with the D139. Turn left here and the grotte is at the end. The distance from Veyreau to the grotte is 9km (5.5 miles).

Discovered in 1880 by a young Shepherd, Grotte de Dargilan is absolutely stunning! The cave is one of the largest in Europe, still active, and has an amazing range of stalactites and stalagmites. It is often referred to as La Grotte Rose (the Pink Cave). The only way to view the cave, which is essentially on two levels, is on a guided tour which lasts about an hour. From the entrance a passage leads into a huge underground chamber, 140m long, 50m wide and 25m high, and from there, the second part of the tour on a lower level is along a deep river passage. (Note: the view from the café area of the Gorges de la Jonte is spectacular)

If you decide to visit Aven Armand as well (**GPS: N44.22113 E3.35731**), or instead of Grotte de Dargilan, the best way of getting there is from Meyrueis as it's only about 11.5km (7 miles) from here. Come out on the D986 heading north, and after 9.3 km (5.7 miles) at the crossroads turn left – it's signposted from here.

Since its discovery in 1897 by Louis Armand and subsequent public opening in 1927, Aven Armand on the Causse Méjean has become one of the most visited places in the region. The central cavern (Aven in French means cavern) is some 75 metres high and contains over 400 palmtrunc stalagmites, the largest being around 30 metres high and claimed to be the tallest one in the world. There is a funicular (tunnel train) that runs down into the cave. All visits to the cave are by guided tour, which costs about €9.

Mont Aigoual, Cirque de Navacelles

As always in this area, the majority of rides are along spectacular, scenic roads, and the route to Mont Aigoual (**GPS:** N44.12144 E3.58000) in the Cévennes is no exception. There are two different ways of getting there, and the northern route is preferred to avoid some duplication of roads on the return journey. Mont Aigoual is 26km (16 miles away) from Meyrueis and navigating there is simple. Take the D996 out of Meyrueis heading north east as if you were going to Florac – this is the road you came in on. After 11km (6.8 miles) turn off right onto the D18, and then 13km (8 miles) later turn left onto the D118 leading to the top of the mountain.

Located in the Gard département, Mont Aigoual, at 1567 metres high, offers dramatic views of south east France on a clear day. The summit is quite large with plenty of parking spaces, an excellent café, and an observatory. This meteorological observatory was built in 1887 and is currently used by Météo France. It is now the only weather station in France still inhabited by meteorologists. There is also a small exhibition here on weather forecasting together with a collection of old and new instruments.

Leave the mountain on the D269 (come out of the car park the same way you came in but at the exit point turn right, not left onto the D118) and begin the descent down the mountain. Keep bearing left on the descent and when you come to a 'T' junction turn left onto the D986 becoming the D48 down to Le Vigan. The roads from Mont Aigoual to Le Vigan, around 35km (22 miles) down through the Hérault Valley, are superb.

Pont d'Arc, Gorges de l'Ardèche

It's not a fast road, but very twisty, with many continuous tight bends, but almost throughout you're riding through deep forests of beech and chestnut woods which are very picturesque on a sunny day.

Le Vigan is a good place to stop for lunch before riding further south to the Cirque de Navacelles. The Place du Quai has some good cafés and restaurants which is found near the centre (**GPS : N43.99119 E3.60685** approx.).

To reach the Cirque de Navacelles (**GPS: N43.89527 E3.50687**) from Le Vigan i.e. the viewpoint in the north looking down on the Cirque to the south, you need to take the D48 and head south to Montdardier. Go through Montdardier, still on the D48, and after 1.6km (1 mile) turn right onto the D413 to Blandas. After 7.2km (4.4 miles) turn left at the village onto the D113 and follow the signs for the Cirque which is only a short distance away. The Cirque de Navacelles can be viewed from the other side of the ravine, from La Baume-Auriol, but the north view is chosen as it's just as good as the southern aspect and much easier to get to.

Looking down at the Cirque and along the Gorges de la Vis, east to west, from the viewpoint is a real 'wow'! You are able to vividly see how, millions of years ago, a river channel cut through the valley and created an oxbow lake. The River Vis, over time, continued to erode which is why the dried up oxbow lake sits above the final cut channel in the valley floor below. The deposits of silt and peat left in the lake when it dried up have created a very fertile area of arable land. There are several small settlements on the edge of the dried up lake, and it is possible to ride down there from Blandas with extreme care.

Much of the journey back to Meyrueis retraces your outward route. Come out of the Cirque and back on the D48 to Le Vigan via Montdardier. Remain on the D48 going around the west side of Le Vigan and then all the way back up until you come across the D986 at L'Espérou where you turn left for the remaining 26km (16 miles) to Meyrueis. The distance from Montdardier to L'Espérou is about 35km (22 miles).

Gorges de l'Ardèche

As stated earlier, this is a ride out and back of some 372km (231 miles) and will take all day to complete, largely because there is no realistic direct route to the gorges and a lot of the roads (whilst largely stunning) are twisty and slow. There are few fast sections on the route out (except parts of the N106) until you reach Alès and head north on the D904. You should allow at least 10 hours for the ride, including fuel, breaks and photo stops.

Leave Meyrueis on the D996 then D907 to Florac, about 33km (20.5 miles). At the edge of the town turn right onto the N106 all the way to Alès, a distance of some 94km (58.4 miles). This road gives you a chance to experience some of the scenery along the northern part of the Cévennes. Don't go into Alès but take the second exit at the first roundabout on the outskirts of the town (**GPS:** N44.14575 E4.06794), and onto the ring road. After about 3km (1.8 miles) turn left onto the D904 becoming the D104 to St-Ambroix and Aubenas. Ride for about 34km (21 miles) then bear right onto the D111 for 11km (6.8 miles) before turning right onto the D579 to Vallon-Pont-d'Arc. As you enter the village turn right onto the D290 which is the road that takes you the length of the Gorges de l'Ardèche (**GPS:** N44.40777 E4.38715).

From Vallon-Pont-d'Arc to almost the end of the gorges at St-Martin-d'Ardèche is 36km (22.3 miles). The whole route is spectacular with lots of tight hairpin bends and a few tunnels as you descend down the gorges along the Ardèche River. You come to one of the main highlights of the route very quickly, after just 4km (2.4 miles), the Pont d'Arc. This is an amazing arch, left as a result of the Ardèche River cutting through the limestone rock. It's a very popular spot for tourists, and in the holiday season it's packed out with canoes on the river. There is a viewpoint at a car park very near the waters edge as you approach the arch. A better view though is a little further along the D290, around the long bend as you slightly ascend. There is an excellent lay-by on your right here where you can safely park the bike and take some more photographs, this time looking slightly down and through the arch.

The rest of the ride down to St-Martin-d'Ardèche (**GPS:** N44.30138 E4.56503) is equally impressive, and if you are keen to stop and take in the views you will find many safe places to pull in to.

The easiest way back to Meyrueis is to retrace the route you came out on.

DAY 8

This is the ride back up to the northern part of the Massif Central, to Châtelguyon, which is located to the west side of the A71-E11 motorway (Meyrueis was to the east). Apart from the last section, the route retraces the superb roads you came down on originally, up as far as the A89-E70 motorway.

The last section starts at Junction 2 with the D906 and the A89-E70 motorway, just north of Pont-de-Dore. Join the motorway here heading west to Clermont-Ferrand, on the outskirts turning right and heading north up the A71-E11 coming off at Junction 13 for Riom. Châtelguyon is about 21km (13 miles) from here.

DAY 9

Although there is a lot to do in this area the main objective is a ride out to visit the Puy de Dôme (**GPS:** N45.77222 E2.96476).

Firstly, some notes on the area. Clermont-Ferrand, just to the south of Châtelguyon, is located in the Auvergne region and is the capital of the Puy-de-Dôme département. It is essentially an industrial town, where over a hundred years ago the Michelin tyre manufacturing company was formed. Although the company still has its headquarters here, most of the tyres are now made abroad. Most of the area to the north and west, down as far as Aurillac is in the Parc Naturel Régional des Volcans d'Auvergne, France's largest national park. Within this is an area known as Monts-Dômes, containing a number of extinct volcanoes including the Puy de Dôme, 14km (8 miles) west of Clermont, and one of the most prominent.

The Puy de Dôme is 1,464 metres above sea level, and is the highest extinct volcanic plug in the region. A huge television mast and observatory are at the summit, but all-round views of the surrounding area and well beyond are stunning on a good day. After a spiralling ride up through dense woodland you'll find a large car park at the top, with no problems for parking a bike, and good visitor facilities including an excellent café. On the road up you will also see the remains of a Roman temple known as the 'Temple of Mercury' which is open to the public.

Although there is a quicker and more direct route for getting to the Puy de Dôme from Châtelguyon, the suggested route below is far more enjoyable and scenic. Come out of Châtelguyon on the D227, D455 then D986 heading south to Volvic. Go around Volvic on the D986 which becomes the D943 to Pontgibaud. Just before Pontgibaud, at the roundabout, turn left onto the D941 and ride 14.3km (8.8 miles) to the end. At the 'T' junction turn right onto the D942 and after 2km turn right again onto the D68 which takes you to the Puy. From the centre of Châtelguyon to the top of the Puy de Dôme is 49km (30.4 miles).

If you want a different and very pleasant route back, at least to Pontgibaud, then after

Puy de Dôme in the Massif Central, from the D68

descending the Puy follow the D68 back to the main D942. Turn right and ride for 10.3km (6.4 miles). At the roundabout turn right onto the D2089, and ride for another 7.3 km (4.5 miles) before turning right onto the D986 back to Pontgibaud, 12km (7.4 miles) away.

If you opt to go into Clermont-Ferrand itself on the way back then the Cathédrale Notre-Dame and the medieval area around it is the best place to start (**GPS:** N45.77900 E3.08566). Note: if you have Sat/Nav make sure you set your accommodation as your 'home location' before you leave because getting out of Clermont-Ferrand is not easy! If you don't have sat/nav follow signs for Riom and the D2009 north.

DAYS 10 & 11

Day 10 is the ride back to Chenonceaux, and day 11 is the ride back to Caen and the Ouistreham Ferry Terminal. The routes back are the same as the outward ones.

Suggested Places to Stay...

CHENONCEAUX

HOTELS

Hôtel Restaurant La Roseraie
7 rue de Docteur Bretonneau,
37150 Chenonceaux
Tel: +33 (0)2 47 23 90 09
Fax: +33 (0)2 47 23 91 59
Email: sfiorito@wanadoo.fr
Web: http://www.hotel-chenonceau.com
GPS: N47.33210 E1.06659

Notes: Located in the main high street at Chenonceaux (on the D40). Stayed here many times. Highly recommend, they don't come any better. Owned by Sophie and Laurent, both of whom speak excellent English. Laurent is a biker (got a BMW but doesn't have the time to use it much). Private secure parking locked at night – bike can go undercover. Very good rooms. Small swimming pool, nice bar, and very good breakfasts. 18 Rooms, from €53. Château Chenonceaux is a 3 minute walk away.

Hôtel Restaurant Le Relais
10 rue de Docteur Bretonneau,
37150 Chenonceaux
Tel: +33 (0)2 47 23 98 11
Fax: +33 (0)2 47 23 84 07
Email: info@chenonceaux.com
Web: http://www.chenonceaux.com/uk
GPS: N47.33195 E1.06679

Notes: Located in the main high street at Chenonceaux (on the D40), almost opposite the Hôtel Restaurant La Roseraie. Stayed here several times and it's quite acceptable. English is well spoken by several of the staff. Bike can either be left on the front courtyard or in a locked garage at night. Good restaurant. 24 Rooms, from €50.

CAMPING

Campsite le Moulin Fort
37150 Francuil-Chenonceaux
(just off the D80)
Tel: +33 (0)2 47 23 86 22
Fax: +33 (0)2 47 23 80 93
Email: lemoulinfort@wanadoo.fr
Web: http://www.lemoulinfort@wanadoo.fr
GPS: N47.32693 E1.08577

Notes: Opening season from 1st April to 30th September inclusive. 137 touring pitches; total area 3 hectares. Château Chenonceaux is approximately 1 km away. This is a British owned camp site, very friendly and accommodating. Stayed here several times, and it is an excellent place to camp, right alongside the River Cher, with good facilities.

B&B

Le Clos Mony
6 rue des Bleuets, 37150 Chenonceaux
Tel: +33 (0)2 47 23 82 68
Email: clos.mony@wanadoo.fr
Web: www.france-bonjour.com/clos-mony/
GPS: N47.33309 E1.06962

Notes: Contact is Betty le Clainche. Open all year. Rooms from €49. 19th century farmhouse offering three rooms, with an additional two rooms available in a house opposite the farmyard. All rooms have bathroom or WC and shower. Private parking available.

MARINGUES

HOTEL

Hôtel Restaurant Le Clos Fleuri
18 route de Clermont, 63350 Maringues
Tel: +33 (0)4 73 68 70 46
Fax : +33 (0)4 73 68 75 58
Email: closfleuri63@wanadoo.fr

Web: http://www.leclosfleuri.net
GPS: N45.91294 E3.33276

Notes: Closed 7th February to 7th March and 25th July to 1st August. 14 rooms from €50. Excellent hotel for an overnight stop. Very good rooms, nice restaurant. Plenty of covered parking for bikes well to the rear of the hotel, not locked but acceptably secure.

CAMPING

Camping Le Pont-Astier
Base de Loisirs, 63190 Orléat / Pont-Astier
Tel: +33 (0)4 73 53 64 40
Fax: +33 (0)3 21 81 47 91
Email: bgressier@nordnet.fr
Web: http://www.camping-lepont-astier.fr
GPS: N45.86783 E3.47606

Notes: Opening season from 1st May to 30th September inclusive. 91 pitches; total area 3.5 hectares. Located on the D224 road between Maringues and Pont-de-Dore (3.3km / 2 miles from Pont-de-Dore).

B&B

La Fermette
Domaine du Casson,
63310 St-Priest-Bramefant
Tel: +33 (0)4 70 59 08 56
Fax: +33 (0)4 70 59 08 56
Email: la-fermette@club-internet.fr
Web: http://rembertmichele.club.fr/lafermette/index.html
GPS: N46.02855 E3.44011 (approx.)

Notes: Contact Michèle and Francis Roche. Located about 18km (11 miles) north east of Maringues. Adjoining the owner's house, this old farmhouse offers one twin room, and three doubles. All rooms have WC with bath or shower facilities.

MEYRUEIS

HOTELS

Hôtel Restaurant Le Family
Quai de la Barrière, 48150 Meyrueis
Tel: +33 (0)4 66 45 60 02
Fax: +33 (0)4 66 45 66 54
Email: hotel.family@wanadoo.fr
Web: http://www.hotel-family.com
GPS: N44.17727 E3.42842

Notes: Located in the main street, the D986 road. Excellent position, close to some very good bars and restaurants. 48 rooms from €44. There is a large and very secure garage with an electric operated door just around the corner from the hotel, and the last time I stayed here I was given the key to retain during my stay. Rooms are good. The hotel restaurant is OK, but I preferred the less formal restaurants just down the road where there is a good choice.

Hôtel du Mont Aigoual
34 Quai de la Barrière, 48150 Meyrueis
Tel: +33 (0)4 66 45 65 61
Fax: +33 (0)4 66 45 64 25
Email: hotelmontaigoual@free.fr
Web: http://www.hotel-mont-aigoual.com
GPS: N44.17620 E3.42902

Notes: Located in the main street, the D986 road, just a little further along from the Hôtel Family. Excellent position as above. 28 rooms from €57. Parking available.

CAMPING

Camping Caravanning le Champ d'Ayres
Route de la Brèze, 48150 Meyrueis
Tel: +33 (0)4 66 45 60 51
Email: campinglechampdayres@wanadoo.fr
Web: http://campinglechampdayres.com
GPS: N44.18075 E3.43524

Notes: Located just to the east of Meyrueis on the road out to Château d'Ayres, 8 minutes walking from the centre of town. Opening season from 11th April to 19th September. 85 touring pitches; total area 1.5 hectares. Excellent site at an altitude of about 700m. Also have Chalets and mobile homes for hire.

Camping la Cascade
Salvinsac, 48150 Meyrueis
Tel: +33 (0)4 66 45 45 45
Email: contact@camping-la-cascade.com
Web: http://www.camping-la-cascade.com
GPS: N44.19688 E3.45808

Notes: Opening season from 15th April to 30th September. 37 touring pitches; total area 1 hectare at an altitude of 782m. Located on the D996 Meyrueis to Florac road clearly signposted (about 3.6km / 2.2 miles) out of Meyrueis. Chalets available.

B&B

La Mosaïque Chambre d'hôtes
Gatuzieres, 48150 Meyrueis
Tel: +33 (0)4 66 45 64 10 or +33 (0)6 74 58 28 85
Email: tresjlm@aol.com
Web: http://www.causses-cevennes.com/gatuzieres
GPS: N44.19877 E3.48859

Notes: Located in a tiny hamlet just off the D966 Meyrueis to Florac road, 6km (3.7 miles) from the centre of Meyrueis. Open from March to November. Contact Muriel Trescarte. Next door to the owners, this gite offers three bedrooms, two with a double and two single beds and one with a double bed. All rooms have private bathroom and WC.

CHÂTELGUYON

HOTELS

L'Hôtel de Paris
1 rue Docteur Levadoux, 63140 Châtelguyon
Tel: +33 (0)4 73 86 00 12
Fax: +33 (0)4 73 86 43 55
Email: hotel.de.paris@wanadoo.fr
Web: http://www.hoteldeparis-chatelguyon.com
GPS: N45.91969 E3.06543

Notes: Located just off the main street (D78) running through the town. 59 rooms from €37. Private garages (no doors) at the back of the hotel for bikes. Quite an old hotel but fine for an overnight stop. Large bedrooms.

Hôtel Régence Central
31 ave des Etats-Unis, 63140 Châtelguyon
Tel: +33 (0)4 73 86 02 60
Fax: +33 (0)4 73 86 12 49
Email: hotel-regence3@wanadoo.fr
Web: http://www.hotel-regence-central.com
GPS: N45.91938 E3.07025

Notes: Located on the main street (D78) running through the town. Open from 21st March to 29th October. 17 rooms from €50. Private, covered parking available.

CAMPING

Camping Clos de Balanède
Route de la Piscine, 63140 Châtelguyon
Tel: +33 (0)4 73 86 02 47
Fax: +33 (0)4 73 86 05 64
Email: clos-balanede.sari-camping@wanadoo.fr
Web: http://www.balanede.com
GPS: N45.91491 E3.07720

Notes: Located just off the D227 as you come into the town. Opening season from 10th April to 1st October inclusive. 280 touring pitches; total area 4 hectares.

B&B

La Treille
25 rue de l'Église, 63200 Davayat
Tel: +33 (0)4 73 63 58 20
Mobile: +33 (0)6 63 90 73 67
Email: honnorat.la.treille@wanadoo.fr
Web: http://honnorat.la.treille.free.fr/uk
GPS: N45.9417 E3.10635 (approx.)

Notes: Contact Nicole and Stephan Honnorat. A 19th century country mansion offering an outbuilding with three double rooms and a suite with two twin bedded rooms. All have WC and bath or shower. From €73. Private parking.

tournumber:9

Cherbourg – Carnac (via Vitré) Carnac – Cherbourg (via Dinan)

SUMMARY

Duration: Minimum 3 days

Cherbourg - Carnac (via Vitré): 388km (241 miles)
Time: 5 hrs 31 mins (riding)
Carnac - Cherbourg (via Dinan): 363km (225 miles)
Time: 5 hrs 3 mins (riding)

TOUR OVERVIEW

This is the third of the three tours to Brittany, the others being Tour 1 to Dinan in the north east, and Tour 4 to St Pol-de-Léon in the north west. This one takes you to Carnac in the far south of Brittany (Bretagne), the base for exploring and riding around the region. Three days is the minimum for this tour because two are taken up with getting there and back, and at least one day is needed to explore, preferably more because there is so much to see in this region.

Carnac is the chosen base for touring southern Brittany because of its proximity to some beautiful rugged coastline and some lovely towns and villages, most of them medieval. Carnac itself, although primarily a tourist town, is nevertheless very pleasant, and is at the centre of some amazing megalithic monuments that go back over 4,000 years BC.

The route down to Carnac from the ferry terminal at Cherbourg takes you via St-Lô, Fougères, Vitré and Vannes. Allowing for stops, the journey will take around 7-8 hours along some good roads, so a relatively early start is needed from Cherbourg. No motorways are used on the route, but there is a section of dual carriageway from Cherbourg (N13) to the turn off for St-Lô of some 48km (30 miles), then 14km (8.6 miles) around St-Lô, and finally a section just before Vannes in the south to Auray of 30km (19 miles). There is of course a quicker route down to Carnac via Rennes, but it's all motorway and dual carriageway.

The main beach at Quiberon

The return ride to Cherbourg follows a different route back but just as enjoyable, via Josselin to Dinan, then onto Avranches and straight up the Cherbourg peninsula to the port to catch the ferry back. Of course, if you have the time then an overnight stay at Dinan is an option, in which case refer to Tour 1 for accommodation suggestions, also 'What to do when you get there'.

ROUTE DESCRIPTION – CHERBOURG TO CARNAC

The route down to Carnac is 388km (241 miles) and is predominately across country through some beautiful historic towns and villages. From the Cherbourg ferry terminal get onto the N13-E46 dual carriageway to Bayeux, Caen, and Paris. This takes you down the Cherbourg peninsula and out eastwards, around Valognes, and a little further along before turning off right and onto the N174 to St-Lô. There is a fairly new dual carriageway which bypasses the town to the south (still the N174). Leave the bypass here and take the D999 down to Percy and Villedieu-les-Poêles. The D999 to Villedieu (crossing over the main A84-E401 motorway) is mostly a fast, straight road, but after Villedieu it becomes much more scenic and a much better ride, with many good bends interspersed with fast straight sections.

The D999 ends just before St-Hilaire-du-Harcouët. Go through the town and out due south on the straight D977 becoming the D177 to Fougères, 25km (15.5 miles) away. The last section going through the Forêt de Fougères just before the ring road is quite pleasant, and the pretty woodlands contain a number of Neolithic monuments. On reaching Fougères (**GPS: N48.35431 W1.20021**) you will have ridden around 177km (110 miles), and although the designated route takes you around the town it's actually a convenient place to stop off for a break. Fougères is a strategic, heavily fortified town at the extreme edge of the Bretagne (Brittany) region, in the Ille-de-Vilaine département. The main attraction in the town is Château de Fougères, a medieval castle and one of the largest in Europe, built on a large area of granite rock which dominates the town. The town is on two levels, separated by imposing cliffs, and altogether it's very picturesque.

Low tide at Carnac-Plage

From Fougères head south, initially on the D798 then D178 to Vitré, 30km (19 miles) away. Again, the route takes you on the ring road around the town, but this is an excellent alternative stop to Fougères if you wish to head into the centre for a break. Vitré is a market town and one of the finest preserved medieval towns in Brittany, a rival even to Dinan in the north of the region. There are many narrow, cobbled streets here with numerous half-timbered houses, cafés, restaurants and bars. The fortified castle, with its many turrets and associated ramparts, is very picturesque (**GPS : N48.12424 W1.21446**).

Take the D777 out of Vitré to Janzé, and from there onto Bain-de-Bretagne crossing over the N137-E3 on the D772 to Messac and Guipry. From Guipry the road becomes the D777 to Pipriac and La Gacilly. Vitré to La Gacilly is approx. 90km (56 miles). La Gacilly is a very pretty, small town on the River Aff, with many narrow streets housing artisans' workshops offering high quality gifts and decorative items. It is also the headquarters of the major cosmetic company Yves Rocher.

Continue on the D777, which is a twisty

but scenic road, heading east, skirting just to the north of Rochefort-en-Terre, which is worth a small diversion to ride through if nothing else, because it's one of the most delightful villages in the whole of Brittany (**GPS : N47.69936 W2.33735**). Apart from a number of fine 17th century houses in the main street, the village has a partly restored medieval fortress, although most of it still remains in ruins. The village is also extensively covered, in season, with huge displays of colourful geraniums.

From Rochefort continue to the end of the D777 before turning right onto the main D775, a fast and predominately straight road leading to the N166 dual carriageway to Vannes. From Vannes join the N165-E60 to Auray before coming off to join the D768 then D781 to Carnac. Vannes to Carnac is about 39km (24 miles).

WHAT TO DO WHEN YOU GET THERE

The southern Morbihan and south west Finistère départements of the Bretagne region are extremely popular areas for tourists, and justifiably so. Unless you are able to spend several weeks here then you can't hope to visit all the attractions. As with some of the other tours, I've tried to highlight below some of the more appealing attractions that also offer the chance to get some good riding in as well. In general, the roads in the area are very good although some of the coastal ones could do with some resurfacing work.

Carnac and Quiberon

Extremely popular with holiday-makers (particularly British) in the summer season, the seaside part of Carnac (Carnac-Plage) with its many sandy beaches, overlooks the Baie de Quiberon, with the town of Quiberon itself at the eastern side of the long peninsula as you look out to the south west. Whilst very much a tourist town, Carnac is nevertheless a very pleasant place to stay

Hôtel Novotel Carnac (left) and Hôtel Ibis Carnac Thalassa

in, well kept and maintained, with a host of good restaurants and cafés to choose from.

However, Carnac's main historic attraction is just to the north, known as the alignments of Carnac, essentially rows of prehistoric standing stones (menhirs), over 3,000 of them in total. Hewn from local rock, most of the megaliths are thought to have been erected between 4500 and 2000 BC. In addition to the rough lines of stones, there are some arranged in circles and some that have other stones placed on top of them. In total, the alignments run for over 4km and can be found along the D196 (Route des Alignments). More information can be found at the visitors centre on the D196, the Maison des Mégalithes (**GPS : N47.59144 W3.08398** approx.) where models of the sites can be viewed and maps etc. are available.

The town of Quiberon (**GPS: N47.48557 W3.11913**), as mentioned earlier, is on the extreme south of a narrow peninsula that juts out into the Baie de Quiberon to the east and the Atlantic Ocean to the west. The peninsula is around 14km (8.6 miles) long, with the start of it just a short 5km (3 miles) from Carnac. It is predominately

Cathédrale St-Corentin, Quimper

built-up, and becomes highly populated in July and August. There are some excellent camp sites and beach walks around, and numerous hotels, bars, cafés and restaurants particularly along the sandy beach near the town to the east. Riding on the peninsula is good, although the main road running through, the D768, can be very busy towards the end (a good time to be on two wheels!). Parking for bikes, as usual, is not a problem. Port Maria on the southernmost tip of the peninsula is a pleasant place to stop. As a suggestion, park your bike outside the Hôtel Albatros and pay a visit to Le Cosaire Restaurant-Bar at the front, and sit outside enjoying an excellent café au lait or beer whilst viewing the long curved sandy beach to your left! (**GPS:** N47.47905 W3.12338).

It's also worth mentioning that Port Maria is where the ferries depart for the islands of Houat, Belle-Île, and Hoëdic. Belle-Île is by far the largest and about 45 minutes away by ferry, but to really appreciate the island you need to spend a day there to make it worthwhile.

Vannes and the Golfe du Morbihan

Vannes is the capital town of the Morbihan département located at the head of the Golfe du Morbihan, some 22km (13 miles) east of Carnac. It is a lovely town and well worth a visit, particularly Vieux Vannes, the old walled but small medieval part which starts at the gates and ramparts at Porte St-Vincent. A few metres south of the gates is Place Gambetta, which is at the top end of the port that gives access out into the Golfe du Morbihan. Parking your motorbike around here (**GPS:** N47.65401 W2.75830) is ideal for walking into the bustling and lively old town (much of it now pedestrianised), and to the Cathédrale St-Pierre and the lovely views from Place Henri-IV just to the left of the church (**GPS:** N47.65759 W2.75768). The main Port area is to the south of the main town, which has hundreds of yachts and other boats moored up. It's worth going down to the Île de Conleau (**GPS:** N47.63050 W2.78053) for the sandy beaches and views, likewise the D199 down to Séné and then Montssarac (**GPS:** N47.59046 W2.72032).

The best route to Vannes from Carnac is to take the coast road out along Carnac-Plage before joining the D781 then D28 up to Auray. Avoid the N165 to Vannes south of Auray as there is a prettier option along the D101, which follows the northern coastline of the Golfe. Go straight into Auray on the D28 and at the first major roundabout take the first exit off into rue de la Terre Rouge, following this down to another major roundabout where again you take the first exit off and onto the D101, to Bono and Vannes.

By going to Vannes you will have covered most of the west and north areas of the Golfe du Morbihan. However, it's still worth coming out of Vannes to ride around the eastern and southern sides as well, to Port-Navalo (**GPS:** N47.54864 W2.91679), which will complete the tour of the Golfe.

Leave Vannes either heading out east on the main N165 dual carriageway, or the D777 leading onto the N165, and turn right and onto the D780 to Noyalo, St-Armel, Sarzeau and Port-Navalo. If the sun is out it's a very enjoyable and relaxing ride!

A few words here on the Golfe du Morbihan itself. The Golfe is connected to the Atlantic Ocean by a very narrow channel between two peninsulas, with the villages of Port-Navalo on one side and Locmariaquer on the west side. Within the Golfe, which is extremely popular with boat owners, are numerous small islands and a number of megalithic sites. The most impressive one is on the Island of Gravrinis which has an 8 metre high tumulus, a Neolithic monument constructed around 3500 BC. The tomb (a large chamber) is built from around 50 stone slabs decorated with carvings, and is reached by a 14 metre long passage. On the Île-d'Arz there are also a number of standing stones. Île-aux-Moines (Monks' Island), which used to be owned by a monastery, is the largest in the Golfe. All three islands can be visit by boat tours that go around the Golfe, departing from Vannes, Port-Navalo, Locmariaquer, Lamor-Baden and Bono. Locmariaquer (**GPS:** N47.57137 W2.94780), mentioned above, is famous for its Fairies' Stone, a huge and broken menhir originally 20 metres high.

The distance from Carnac Plage to Port-Navalo is about 57km (35 miles).

Quimper, Bénodet, Concarneau, Pont-Aven, Lorient

This is almost a complete circular tour from Carnac, taking the direct and fast route straight up to Quimper and then coming slowly back on the roads on or close to the coast, taking in the villages/towns of Bénodet, Concarneau, Pont-Aven and Lorient. The total distance is around 249km (154 miles), which given the different types of roads means about 4 hours riding, so with stops along the route it means a full day out.

Leave Carnac to join the N165-E60 just to the north of Lorient via the D781, D9 then D194. Head out west on the N165 dual carriageway to Quimper, which to the centre is about 104km (65 miles) away. Quimper is a very attractive and pretty city, in a valley at the confluence of the Rivers Odet and Steir. It is the capital of the Finistère département, and it's worth spending an hour or so here exploring. Aim for the old town and the huge Cathédrale St-Corentin. The easiest way from the N165 is to ignore the first junction to the south of the city (the D365) and take the next junction, heading into the centre on the D15. You can't miss the Cathédrale with its twin spires, so look for a suitable place to park the motorbike close by as the medieval part of Quimper should be top of your agenda, and it all starts on the cobbled streets to the west of the church. If you have Sat/Nav aim for **GPS:** N47.99495 W4.10265. Note that much of the medieval sector is now closed to traffic and is pedestrianised. The Cathédrale itself is at **GPS:** N47.99576 W4.10309 along rue Du Roi Gradlon (from the River Odet) leading into Place St-Corentin.

The cobbled streets and the half-timbered buildings are delightful from the Cathédrale, particularly if you walk along rue Kéréon (in front of the church) and the streets that branch off it. Just to the south, the River Odet is crossed by many small bridges, which are very colourful in the spring and summer months, and you are spoilt for choice on places to eat and drink. Quimper is also famous for its production of hand-painted ceramics (faïence), and is offered for sale just about everywhere!

When you can drag yourself away leave Quimper on the road south (essentially following the River Odet) to Bénodet, the D34. It's only a 17km (10.5 mile) ride, but nonetheless, very pleasant. At the second roundabout as you come into the town bear right onto Avenue de l'Odet and follow the road around. You're nearly half way around the town at **GPS:** N47.87416 W4.11016. Bénodet is really a family holiday resort, extremely popular, with a number of very large campsites such as Yelloh! Village Port de Plaisance (entrance as you come in on the D34), Du Poulquer and Du Letty. The harbour here is very pretty with numerous boats, and there are some good seafood restaurants and crêperies around.

From Bénodet it's out on the D44 then D783 heading east, through La Forêt-Fouesnant to Concarneau, a mere 25km (15.5 miles). Although Concarneau is the third largest fishing port in France, it's now also a major tourist town, not least of all because of Ville Close, the fortified old town built on a rocky island that stretches out into the harbour. Access is across a drawbridge, and with the ramparts (built in the 17th century) and the very attractive buildings in the pedestrianised main street, the setting is superb! The ramparts, which you can walk along and enjoy some lovely views of the boats in the harbour and beyond, are illuminated at night. (Note: it gets very crowded here in July and August). The entrance to Ville Close is at **GPS:** N47.87134 W3.91706. Concarneau is also a ville fleurie, and the flowers around the town in summer, particularly those in Ville Close, make the place even more picturesque.

Leave Concarneau on the D783 and ride the 16km (10 miles) to Pont-Aven, a lovely port and town split by the River Aven that flows out to the estuary and the Atlantic beyond. The D783 is the only main road through the port. Originally, the port was renowned for its dozen or more watermills, but only four remain now, one of which, Le Moulin du Grand Poulguin, has become a very popular crêpe and pizza restaurant. However, from the latter part of the 19th century, Pont-Aven become famous for its art galleries and artists, a result of Paul Gauguin and Émile Bernard coming here to paint in the 1880's, joined later by Paul Sérusier, all of whom were the inspiration behind the Pont-Aven School for artists. Just to the north of the port is the Bois d'Amour woodlands and gardens, which inspired Gauguin and hundreds of artists and poets ever since.

From Port-Aven leave on the D783 and head east again before turning south east on the D24 down to Clohars-Carnöet. Here you need to come out on the D224, through the bottom part of the Forêt-de- Carnöet (a lovely stretch of road), before joining the D162 into Guidel. Now you can turn left here and go into Lorient, or alternatively, if you have the time, take the very pretty coastal route by turning right at Guidel and onto the D306 to Guidel-Plages (**GPS:** N47.77147 W3.52678). From here turn left onto the D152, and enjoy the 15km (9 miles) of riding before reaching the outskirts of Lorient, and the D29 that takes you over the bridge and into the city.

Lorient, in the Morbihan département of Bretagne, is a large city and port at the mouths of the Rivers Scorff and Blavet, with the River Le Ter entering the bay from the south east. Bombed extensively during World War II because of the German U-boat base at Keroman to the south of the city, Lorient was almost completely destroyed. The city was rebuilt after the war, particularly in the 1950's, and became a fishing port, commercial centre and a naval base, particularly for the French nuclear submarine fleet. The French Navy, however, is no longer here, and the city today is more of a commercial and administrative centre, with tourism becoming increasingly important to the economy. The town's yachting harbour is also very lively.

The main tourist attraction is the submarine pens at the former U-boat base at Keroman, which is open to the public year round (**GPS:** N47.72781 W3.36674).

By coming in on the D29, navigating to Keroman is easy. As soon as you have crossed the bridge (over the River Le Ter) take an immediate right and follow the road round to the left to the roundabout, where you take the first exit off. The submarine base is just down the road; it's very well signposted.

Also well worth mentioning is the Inter-Celtic Festival held in Lorient each year in August, which attracts thousands of visitors from all the European Celtic nations www.festival-interceltique.com.

Getting out of Lorient through the main town and back to Carnac, without the use of Sat/Nav, can be challenging! However, if you've opted to go to the U-boat base and are heading straight back to Carnac then it's very easy. It's about 38km (24 miles). Go back to the main roundabout you came in on (to get to the base), and go straight ahead and onto the D465, which conveniently takes you all the way round to join the main N165 dual carriageway. Head east, to Auray and Vannes, then come off at the first junction after crossing over the bridge and the River Blavet, and turn right onto the D781. At the first roundabout turn left onto the D194 to Carnac. If you have Sat/Nav and have forgotten to set your accommodation to 'Home', then **GPS: N47.58438 W3.08226** will at least take you to the outskirts of Carnac.

ROUTE DESCRIPTION – CARNAC TO CHERBOURG

As mentioned in the 'Tour Overview' notes at the beginning, the return journey back to Cherbourg is via Josselin and Dinan, a slightly more direct route than the one you came down on, and marginally shorter. Nevertheless, it's still a ride of 363km (225 miles), and if you are booked on the evening ferry from Cherbourg to Poole you need to

Ville Close, Concarneau

Menhirs at Carnac

arrive at the port by 17:45 hrs for the 18:30 departure (Sunday, Monday, Wednesday, and Friday only). With stops it could take you around 7-8 hours to complete, a touch longer if you stop off for an hour or so at Josselin, but still plenty of time as long as you don't leave too late!

Leave Carnac on the D781 then D28 up to Auray to join the N165 dual carriageway to Vannes, then take the D767 to Locminé, Pontivy and Josselin. After just 6.6km (4 miles) you take a right onto the D778, through the villages of St-Jean-Brévelay and Guéhenno, until you reach the main N24 dual carriageway. Join the N24 and ride the short distance to Josselin. If you decide not to stop in the town then come off the N24 to the north and take the D793 which takes you almost to the N176-E401 just short of Dinan. At Josselin you will have travelled 79km (49 miles).

Josselin is located in the Morbihan département of the Bretagne region, in a lovely setting on the River Oust. The Josselin château, with its three large round towers overlooking the Oust, dominates the town and is one of the main attractions. The castle, built by the Rohan family who still inhabit it, has had a chequered history having been partly destroyed and rebuilt at various times between the 11th and 17th centuries, until being extensively restored in the 19th. It's possible to visit the château and the gardens between April and September. Elsewhere, the town is very medieval with many 16th century half timbered buildings together with the gargoyled Notre-Dame-du-Roncier basilica overlooking the town centre. There are many nice cafés and restaurants around. (**GPS: N47.95409 W2.54797**)

You leave Josselin on the D793 heading due north for the next 73km (45 miles) up to the main N176-E401 dual carriageway. There is nothing particularly special about the D793, but it's a good road that passes through some quite pleasant villages. Once on the N176 / N175 heading for St-Malo, Le Mont-St-Michel and Avranches, you stay on it for about 64km (40 miles) until you reach Avranches. If you're running very short of time for the ferry then stay on the N175 which becomes the A84-E3 motorway and come off at Junction 40 for St-Lô and then to Cherbourg. It's nearly all motorway/dual carriageway, about 153km (95 miles), which should take about 80 minutes.

If you're not pushed for time then at Avranches take the D973 off the N175 (it's clearly signposted for Cherbourg) and head initially for Granville, taking the D971 to bypass the town, and then continuing up to Coutances. The route takes you around the town of Coutances, but if you have the time it's well worth diverting off into the centre to view at close hand the Cathédrale de Notre-Dame that dominates the surrounding countryside.

From Coutances take the D2 to Lessay, then D900 to La Haye-du-Puits and St-Sauveur, then the D2 again to Valognes. From here the N13 goes straight up to Cherbourg and the ferry terminal.

Suggested Places to Stay...

HOTELS

Hôtel Ibis Carnac Thalassa
6 Allée Fleur de Sel, 56343 Carnac-Plage
Tel: +33 (0)2 97 52 54 00
Fax: +33 (0)2 97 52 53 66
Web: http://www.ibishotel.com/gb/hotel-1054-ibis-carnac-thalassa/index.shtml
GPS: **N47.57153 W3.08214**

Notes: Very good location, a short walk from Carnac-Plage. 121 rooms from €87 depending on the season. Private car park. Good facilities.

Hôtel An Ti Gwenn
4 rue de Poul Person, 56340 Carnac
Tel: +33 (0)2 97 52 00 73
Fax: +33 (0)2 97 52 81 88
Web: http://www.hotel-antigwenn.com
GPS: **N47.58565 W3.07596**

Notes: Located about 1.5km from the beach at Carnac-Plage. 10 rooms from €55 depending on the season. Private car park. No restaurant here but you can use the one at their other hotel (Hôtel Tumulus) a short walk away.

Hôtel Novotel Carnac
Avenue de l'Atlantique,
56340 Carnac-Plage
Tel: +33 (0)2 97 52 53 00
Fax: +33 (0)2 97 52 53 55
Web: http://www.novotel.com/gb/hotel-0406-novotel-carnac/index.shtml
GPS: **N47.57222 W3.07952**

Notes: Located very close to the Hôtel Ibis in Carnac-Plage. Great hotel with superb facilities, but it's not cheap. 109 rooms from €102. You can sometimes negotiate a good deal though, particularly outside of July/August. Breakfasts are superb, but cost around €15. Hotel is only a short walk from some excellent bars and restaurants, which offer much better value than the Hotel. Own private car park (not locked).

CAMPING

Castel Camping La Grand Métairie
Route des Alignements de Kermario, 56342 Carnac
Tel: +33 (0)2 97 52 24 01
Email: info@lagrandemetairie.com
Web: http://www.lagrandemetairie.com
GPS: **N47.59865 W3.06034**

Notes: Located on the D196 just to the north of Carnac. Open from 28th March to 5th September. Busy, lively site with 149 touring pitches available and good facilities.

Camping des Menhirs
Allée Saint-Michel, 56343 Carnac-Plage
Tel: +33 (0)2 97 52 94 67
Fax: +33 (0)2 97 52 25 38
Email: contact@lesmenhirs.com
Web: http://www.lesmenhirs.com
GPS: **N47.57544 W3.06802**

Notes: Great location, 300m from the beach, and very close to the cafés, bars, restaurants etc. of Carnac-Plage. 350+ pitches. Very good facilities incl. swimming pools etc.

Continued…

B&B

Ker Kristal
12 Kerguearec, 56340 Carnac
Tel: +33 (0) 2 97 56 73 57 or
+33 (0) 6 84 91 43 36
Email: kerkristal@yahoo.fr
Web: http://www.kerkristal.com
GPS: **N47.61642 W3.04746** (approx.)

Notes: Located about 7km north east of Carnac. Contact Jurgen and Jocelyne Heiligtag. Open all year round. Guesthouse offering three guest rooms comprising a twin room, a double with one single and a family room with one double and two singles. From €48. All rooms have ensuite facilities and private garden.

Ty-Me-Mamm
Quelvezin, 56340 Carnac
Tel: +33 (0) 2 97 52 45 87
Email: tymemam@wanadoo.fr
Web: www.gites-de-france-morbihan.com/tymemam
GPS: **N47.63016 W3.08798** (approx.)

Notes: Contact Anne-Sophie Daniel. Restored 1900 farmhouse offering four comfortable guestrooms comprising three doubles and one triple. All rooms have private shower room and WC. From €45.

tournumber:10

Caen – Fontenay-le-Comte – Biscarrosse – Vieux-Boucau – Luz-St-Sauveur – Tarascon-sur-Ariège – Bolquère – Carcassonne – Les Eyzies – Saumur – Caen

SUMMARY

Duration: 10 days minimum

Day 1: **Caen - Fontenay-le-Comte** - 425km (264 miles)
Time: 6 hrs 45 mins (riding)

Day 2: **Fontenay-le-Comte - Biscarrosse** - 347km (215miles)
Time: 4 hrs 44 mins (riding)

Day 3: **Biscarrosse - Vieux-Boucau** - 88km (55 miles)
Time: 1hrs 31 mins (riding)

Day 4: **Vieux-Boucau - Luz-St-Sauveur** - 274km (170 miles)
Time: 6-7 hrs (riding)

Day 5: **Luz-St-Sauveur - Tarascon** - 232km (144 miles)
Time: 5-6 hrs (riding)

Day 6: **Tarascon - Bolquère** - 171km (106 miles)
Time: 3-4 hrs (riding)

Day 7: **Bolquère - Carcassonne** - 204km (126 miles)
Time: 3-4 hours (riding)

Day 8: **Carcassonne - Les Eyzies** - 316km (196 miles)
Time: 4 hrs 18 mins (riding)

Day 9: **Les Eyzies - Saumur** - 292km (182 miles)
Time: 5 hrs 10 mins (riding)

Day 10: **Saumur - Caen** - 236km (147 miles)
Time: 4 hr 30 mins (riding)

TOUR OVERVIEW

This is the longest of the ten tours in this booklet, covering around 2,585km (1,606 miles) in total. The main objective of the tour is to ride across the Pyrénées, from the Atlantic Ocean on the west coast to the Mediterranean in the east i.e. from Biarritz to Perpignan. The planned route across the mountains, which goes through Andorra and briefly into Spain, is a distance of some 687km (426 miles) over a four day period with three overnight stays. If the weather is an issue, and you're on a fixed time-scale, then you won't be able to complete all of the days and/or sections, so you must be prepared for some flexibility and adapt accordingly (more on this later).

Once past the east of Nantes the ride down to the Pyrénées stays very much to the Atlantic coastline of France. There are three overnight stops as you ride down the west coast, at Fontenay-le-Compe, Biscarrosse and Vieux-Boucau. The ride from Biscarrosse to Vieux-Boucau is very short and deliberately so. The stretch of coastline between Arcachon (just to the north of Biscarrosse) and Biarritz in the south has mile upon mile of lovely sandy beaches which is ideal for surfing or just relaxing on the beach. Vieux-Boucau is a particularly good base for this (more later), and a great place to unwind before you face the rigors of the Pyrénées mountains.

The ride across the Pyrénées is extremely challenging in places and not for the inexperienced biker, particularly the section between Laruns and Argelès-Gazost on Day 4, and almost all of Day 5 from Luz-St-Sauveur to Tarascon. Your slow riding ability will be tested to the full! The hazards, which to a greater or lesser extent are relevant to many of the mountainous roads in the Pyrénées, are many. These include very tight, slow hairpin bends, almost always on a sharp ascent or descent, narrow roads with blind bends, loose grit and small stones, long drops off the side of roads with no barriers, other road users (particularly campervans), and freely roaming animals, particularly cattle and sheep, and not least of all their droppings! Riding on these mountain roads can be mentally exhausting because of the sheer amount of concentration required. However, the scenery and stunning views on a clear day from most of the mountain passes are superb, and more than worth the effort needed to get there.

The other hazard when crossing the Pyrénées is often the weather, which can be very unpredictable. There is no point in attempting the crossing between December and March because of the snow. The general consensus is that the weather between September and the end of October, particularly in the east, is more likely to be at its best for riding, with the other benefit that there are far fewer tourists around at this time. It's much wetter in the western half of the Pyrénées because of the influence of the Atlantic, and much drier and hotter in the east because of the Mediterranean high pressure systems. Also bear in mind that at altitude it can be quite cool in the mountains, even in the summer.

Regardless of the time you choose to go make sure you have a contingency plan to hand in case you get caught out in bad weather. The key is flexibility. The main problems I've incurred in the past have been low cloud and drizzle at altitude, the cloud being so dense at times that it's been difficult to make any progress other than at very low speeds. This is more likely to occur in the west. Several times in the past I've had to give up and head north, down the mountains towards the A64 motorway and lower ground, where the weather is often contrastingly sunny!

On Days 4, 5 and 6 there are alternative easier routes (*in blue italics*) to reach the proposed overnight stops in the event of poor weather, particularly useful if you are on a fixed time-scale, and also in case you are not fully confident enough to ride some or all of a particular route. These alternative routes are along good roads and generally quite scenic ones too.

Using campsites across the mountains gives you the greatest flexibility of all because, July and August apart, there's no need to pre-book. Just turn up, and you'll be very unlucky not to get in! Camping can be great fun with a bike! The downside is that you've got to take a certain amount of equipment with you, no real problem if you're touring solo, but it can lead to some interesting discussions before you leave the UK on what to take and what not to take if you're riding two-up! Also, you need to consider the effect the extra load will have on your riding, especially on the tougher parts of some of the routes.

Once across the Pyrénées and around Perpignan it's up to Carcassonne, a lovely city, and from there the route back to Caen takes you to the overnight stops at Les Eyzies in the Dordogne, and Saumur in the Loire Valley.

Camping in the Pyrénées near Tarascon-sur-Ariège

The 10 days suggested for the tour is the minimum if you intend to complete it. You could miss out the overnight stop at Biscarrosse on the way down if you wish, but otherwise it's not really practical to leave out any of the other stops.

ROUTE DESCRIPTION

Day 1

This first day from the Caen ferry terminal down to Fontenay-le-Comte is about 425km (264 miles). The ride down is all across country, and apart from two short sections of motorway, one at the very beginning (A84-E401) and one at the very end (A83), no other motorways are used. Therefore, with fuel and break stops it's a full days' riding, so an early start from Caen, once again, is required.

Coming out of Caen to the ring road via the D514 then D515 is straightforward. To ensure you get onto the A84-E401 motorway follow the signs for Rennes. After 25km (15.5 miles) come off at Junction 42 and take the D577 to Vire. This is a good, fast road through a lot of wooded countryside, and the 27km (16.7 miles) to Vire will go quickly. Go around Vire and on to Mortain, still on the D577, although it changes to the D977 before you get to the town. Mortain (**GPS: N48.64909 W0.94208**) is split by the River Cance, situated on a rocky hill, and was the scene of a major Second World War battle in 1944 when a German Panzer division

The D921 leading down into Luz-St-Sauveur

launched a major counter-attack against American infantry.

From Mortain take the D977 to St-Hilaire-du-Harcouët, and then out on the same road which becomes the D177 to Fougères. The ride through the Forêt de Fougères is very pleasant. On reaching Fougères you will have ridden around 144km (90 miles), and although the designated route takes you around the town it's actually a convenient place to stop off for a break. Fougères (the centre is at **GPS:** N48.35431 W1.20021) is a strategic, heavily fortified town at the extreme edge of the Bretagne (Brittany) region, in the Ille-de-Vilaine département. The main attraction in the town is the Château de Fougères, a medieval castle and one of the largest in Europe, built on a large area of granite rock which dominates the town. The town is on two levels, separated by imposing cliffs, and altogether very picturesque.

From Fougères head south, initially on the D798 then D178 to Vitré, 30km (19 miles) away. Again, this route is the ring road around the town. However, Vitré is an excellent alternative stop to Fougères so follow the signs into the centre if you opt for a break here. Vitré is a market town and one of the finest preserved medieval towns in Brittany, a rival even to Dinan in the north of the region. There are many narrow, cobbled streets here with numerous half-timbered houses, cafés, restaurants and bars. The fortified castle, with its many turrets and associated ramparts, is very picturesque (**GPS :** N48.12424 W1.21446).

Ride around (or through) Vitré and out on the D178 via Martigné-Ferchaud to Châteaubriant, 48km (30 miles) to the south, and from here out to the south east on the D163 to Candé (**GPS:** N47.56206 W1.04267). The D163 is not a spectacular road but it gives you a solid ride and you can make very good progress along it. At the junction on the outskirts of Candé, turn right onto the very straight D923 road down to Ancenis, located on the north bank of the River Loire. At Ancenis you will have covered some 285km (177 miles). If you have not already taken a break, Ancenis is a good place to stop for lunch.

Leave Ancenis by crossing the Loire (**GPS:** N47.36210 W1.17652) and head south on the D763 all the way to Montaigu via Clisson (49km / 30 miles). At Montaigu (**GPS:** N46.98259 W1.30512) take the D137 around the east of the town and out on the road to Chantonnay. After 23km, well before Chantonnay, turn right onto the D160 leading to the A83-E3 motorway. Join the motorway for 53km (33 miles) heading south (to Niort, Saintes, Bordeaux) coming off at Junction 8 and joining the D938 into Fontenay-le-Comte - **GPS:** N46.46487 W0.80226 is the centre.

Day 2

This is the ride from your accommodation at Fontenay-le-Comte to Biscarrosse. Much of the 347km (215 mile) route passes close to or alongside the Atlantic coast, and around the historic towns of La Rochelle, Rochefort and Bordeaux. There is an unavoidable section of motorway in order to get around Bordeaux (A10-E606, A63-E5 and A660) of about 75km (46 miles), but that aside, the ride is most enjoyable, particularly around the coastal towns of Royan and Arcachon.

Leave Fontenay-le-Comte on the D938 south west to Marans, and then turn left onto the D137 then right a little later, onto the N11 to La Rochelle. The N11 takes you a short distance to a major junction to the west of La Rochelle. Turn left here onto the D137 coastal road to Rochefort.

A brief description of La Rochelle and Rochefort follows should you wish to explore either. Both towns however will be covered in considerably more detail in a West Coast tour of France in Edition 2 - to be published at a later date.

La Rochelle is a major, historic port and very picturesque. Like Rochefort, it is located

On the D918 near Barèges

in the Poitou-Charentes region, in the département known as Charente-Maritime. The main focus of the town is the sheltered old harbour (Vieux Port), where there are two towers either side of the entrance and numerous yachts. Head for this area as there is plenty of parking for your motorbike along the harbour walls. **GPS:** **N46.15731 W1.15382** or thereabouts is a good area, close to many cafés and bars, and gives you easy access to some of the medieval areas, much of which is now pedestrianised.

Rochefort, 26km (16 miles) south of La Rochelle, was originally an important French naval base from the 17th to the 19th century. It was built by the military, and as a result has many straight lines of houses and buildings. Nevertheless, parts of the town and the old harbour are very pretty, **GPS:** **N45.93916 W0.95813** near the harbour is a good place to aim for, or alternatively, the Centre International de la Mer alongside the harbour at **GPS:** **N45.94066 W0.95577** is worth going to.

From Rochefort head due south on the D733 to Royan, a distance of 37km (23 miles). Royan (**GPS:** **N45.64076 W1.02492**) is a popular resort with some excellent beaches. Continue around the town on the D25, and out along the coast to Meshers, Talmont and Mortagne. At Meshers the D25 becomes the D145, a lovely ride down the coast on the northern side of the Gironde estuary. The navigable Gironde is some 63km (39 miles) long, and is the main access to Bordeaux for shipping coming in from the Atlantic.

At St-Fort-sur-Gironde (**GPS:** **N45.46197 W0.71909**) take the short D2 to get onto the main D730 to Mirambeau. Mirambeau is the half-way point to Biscarrosse. From there head due south on the D137, bypassing Blaye, all the way down to join the A10-E606 motorway to Bordeaux. The distance from St-Fort to the A10 is 66km (41 miles). The key to getting around Bordeaux (clockwise direction) is to follow signs for Bayonne, which will eventually get you onto the A63-E5 motorway heading south. After 24.5km (15 miles) bear right to join the A660 motorway, then the N250 leading to the south of Arcachon, 30km (19 miles) away.

The proposed route bypasses Arcachon, but if you are not pushed for time then it's well worth the 6km (3.7 mile) ride into in. Arcachon (**GPS:** N44.65908 W1.16438) is a young town, little more than a hundred years old, located in the southern part of the Bassin d'Arcachon which remains open to the Atlantic Ocean. It has an excellent beach, and just to the south is the start of Europe's highest sand dune, the Dune du Pilat. The dune is nearly 3km long, and at 107m above sea level the views from the top are spectacular. In recent years it has become a favourite place for hang gliding enthusiasts. The D218 coast road out of Arcachon to Biscarrosse-Plage takes you along the bottom of the dune to your right.

Biscarrosse-Plage (the coastal resort) is only 29km (18 miles) from Arcachon, and Biscarrosse (the town) just another 9km (5.5 miles) further on. Wherever you decide to stay, it's a relaxing area to be in. The long sandy beach at Biscarrosse-Plage is superb (**GPS:** N44.44518 W1.25527 approx.), and ideal for surfing, but there are also beaches along a nearby lake, the lovely Étang de Cazaux et de Sanguinet (**GPS:** N44.45254 W1.19930), which is nearly 11km long and almost as wide. The coastal area around here is known as the Cote d'Argent. The area from Biarritz in the south all the way up to just beyond Arcachon, and a considerable way inland, is situated in the Landes département, which is in the Aquitaine region. The huge Landes area is situated on land that was reclaimed from the marshes around 200 years ago, and now contains one of the largest forests in Europe, primarily pine trees but also oak and cork. The coastal area and the Landais forests are very popular in the summer months, and there are many good and picturesque roads to ride on throughout this vast region.

Day 3

If the weather is good at Biscarrosse then you might be reluctant to move on down to Vieux-Boucau-les-Baines. However, it's only 88km (55 miles) to this small town and so an early start isn't needed, but it is necessary to

Close to the Col du Tourmalet summit looking west

get further south and nearer to the Pyrénées ready for the 274km (174 mile) ride to Luz-St-Sauveur the following day.

Leave Biscarrosse on the D652 to Parentis and Gastes, then the D87 into Mimizan. Go back onto the D652 out of Mimizan and straight down through the forests, all the way to Vieux-Boucau. If you are camping, and staying at the highly recommended site at Airotel Le Vieux Port, then turn right at the roundabout (by Super U), just before you come into Vieux-Boucau, and the campsite can be found at the end of this road.

Vieux-Boucau (**GPS: N43.78940 W1.39531**) is a very small but attractive town, and quite modern. As at Biscarrosse, the beaches around here are superb for surfing and relaxing on. If you don't want to laze around then Soustons (**GPS: N43.75563 W1.32724**) and the nearby lake are worth a visit, as is the Étang Blanc lake a little to the north of Seignosse.

Day 4

The start of the Pyrénées ride to the overnight stop at Luz-St-Sauveur, so in reality this is Day 1 of the 4 days it takes to cross the mountains, assuming no delays. Check the weather forecast and if it looks reasonable then go for it! What you don't want is low cloud and rain. The run really starts when you join the D932 to the south of Bayonne, and to get there it's a 46km (28.5 mile) ride from the centre of Vieux-Boucau.

Leave Vieux-Boucau on the D652 then turn right onto the D79 to Hossegor and Capbreton. At Capbreton take a left onto the D28 which takes you to Junction 8 of the A63-E5 motorway (it's clearly signposted). Join the motorway southbound (signposted Bayonne, Biarritz) for 22km (13.6 miles) and come off at Junction 5 to join the D932 to Cambo-les-Baines and St-Jean-Pied-de-Port.

At the start of the D932 the altitude is about 150m, but as you progress further along (the D932 becomes the D918), you slowly gain height so that by the time you arrive at St-Jean-Pied-de-Port you've reached close to 600m. The D932 and D918 roads follow the River Nive all the way to St-Jean. The route is quite picturesque, with many hills, and in the distance there is a hint to the east and south of the much higher ground still to come. Both roads are good and easy, and in no way challenging. On arrival at St-Jean (**GPS: N43.16349 W1.23723**) you'll have travelled about 93km (57 miles) of the 274 (170 miles) needed to get to Luz-St-Sauveur, and as St-Jean is quite attractive it's worth stopping for a break here. The town is popular with tourists, and is only a few km from the border with Spain.

From St-Jean travel east on the D933 as far as Larceveau-Arros-Cibits (15km / 9.3 miles), where you turn right at the roundabout and onto the D918 to Mauléon-Licharre. (Note: although there are a few breaks in between, you essentially remain on the D918 all the way through to Argelès-Gazost, which is just 18km to the north of Luz-St-Sauveur).

The road to Mauléon-Licharre (**GPS: N43.21319 W0.89305** - this puts you on the right road out) is twisty in places but otherwise you can make very good progress. The altitude doesn't vary much, between 400 and 500m. Remain on the D918 out of Mauléon heading south to Tardets-Sorholus, where shortly after passing through the village you turn left (still on the D918) towards Aramits and Arrete, which leads on to the main intersection with the N134-E7. The section between Mauléon and the N134 is very hilly in places, and by the time you reach the N134 you're up to around 700m, but it's not an arduous section to ride.

Turn left onto the N134 and ride the short distance up to Asasp, where you turn right, back on the D918 to Arudy and Louvie-Juzon. (Note: on arrival at Asasp you will have covered 171km (106 miles) of the route, leaving 103km (64 miles) to do). The 19km (12 mile) section of the D918 between Asasp and Arudy is the first real challenging road on the route so far, and it requires careful riding. It's very narrow and twisty in places with a few hairpin bends, particularly where you go through the pretty woods of the Bois du Bager. So stay focused!

At Louvie-Juzon turn right and head due south on the D934 for 14km (8.6 miles) to Laruns, where the mountains either side of the town are up to around 1800m. Go through Laruns (**GPS: N42.98647 W0.42686**) and on the outskirts turn left and back on the D918 to Gourette, Col d'Aubisque, Col du Soulor, Arrens-Marsous, and finally Argelès-Gazost.

*Alternative: if the weather is poor, or if you are not sufficiently confident to do the section between Laruns and Argelès-Gazost, which is very demanding, don't go down to Laruns from Louvie-Juzon. Instead, take the D35 out of Louvie-Juzon heading due east to the main D937 Pau - Lourdes road (**GPS: N43.15177 W0.22505**). Turn right, go down to Lourdes, through the town and out south on the D821 to Argelès-Gazost (**GPS: N43.00633 W0.09861**).*

Most of this stretch of the D918 (44km / 27 miles) to Argelès-Gazost is very challenging, and not helped at all in places by the poor quality of the road surface. Last time I rode this in 2008 a lot of the road surface was very bad, and with some extremely long drops down from the side of the road, intense riding concentration is required, especially when there's traffic coming at you from the opposite direction! Having said that, the views and the scenery are absolutely stunning if the weather is good. The twisty road, with some nice bends, rises steadily as you progress along from Laruns, initially on a good surface through the village of Eaux-Bonnes, but by the time you reach the village of Gourette you're already up to 1600m and the road surface deteriorates rapidly after this.

Col d'Aubisque (**GPS: N42.97650 W0.33989**), part of the Tour de France route, is only 4km (2.5 miles) further up from Gourette, at a height of 1709m. There is a café and souvenir shop at the top, and a stop for the views and photos is essential. From here carry on to Col du Soulor which is slightly lower down at 1474m, and then a further descent to the pretty village of Arrens-Marsous, 7.5km (4.6 miles) away.

From Arrens-Marsous it's a comfortable 12km (7.5 mile) ride down to the often congested town of Argelès-Gazost in the Hautes-Pyrénées département of the Midi-Pyrénées region. The town, which is only 13km (8 miles) south of Lourdes (a major tourist / pilgrimage town), is surrounded by high mountains, and has a pleasant main street with plenty of cafés and shops, and well worth stopping for a short break.

Take the D921 out of Argelès, down through the Gorge de Luz, to Luz-St-Sauveur, 18km (11 miles) to the south. If you plan on staying for a day or more at Luz-St-Sauveur then the two places worth going to are Gavarnie and Cauterets / Pont d'Espagne.

The major attraction at Gavarnie (**GPS: N42.73456 W0.01002**), 19km (12 miles) south of Luz, is the Cirque de Gavarnie, a great natural amphitheatre over 1500m high surrounded by cliffs, snow and waterfalls. It's stunning, and well worth the walk down to view it. Cauterets (**GPS: N42.89018 W0.11399**), now a major mountaineering and ski centre located 17km (10.5 miles) south of Argelès-Gazost on the D920, is the gateway leading through the Val de Jéret to Pont d'Espagne. Here, there are a number of spectacular waterfalls cascading down to Cauterets. At the end of the D920 at Pont d'Espagne there is a car park (**GPS: N42.85183 W0.13660**). From here, for a small fee, you can take a ski lift up the mountain and walk through the woods to Lac de Gaube. The lake, at around 1700m, is surrounded by pine forests, and in the distance to the south on the border with Spain is the mighty snow covered Vignemale Mountain at over 3200m. The overall view is breathtaking!

Day 5

This is the second days' riding across the Pyrénées, from Luz-St-Sauveur to Tarascon-sur-Ariège, a distance of 232km (144 miles). Although the distance may not seem very much, in reality it will seem considerably longer. The road surfaces along the route are mainly average, but there are some challenging sections along the way making progress very slow, so with breaks and other stops it will take you all day to complete.

Several of the roads, particularly the D618 from Fronsac to Tarascon-sur-Ariège, are extremely challenging and not for the faint-hearted. Very good slow riding skills are required to get around some of the tight hairpin bends. Strong consideration should be given to spreading this route over two days, stopping off somewhere en route, such as St-Girons. If you are camping then you will have far greater options than if you are staying in hotels or B&Bs.

To summarise, the route takes you from Luz-St-Sauveur along the Col du Tourmalet and Col d'Aspin to Arreau, and from there to Bagnères-de-Luchon, St-Girons and finally Tarascon-sur-Ariège.

*Alternative : Leave Luz-St-Sauveur on the D921 to Argelès-Gazost, then out on the D821 to Lourdes (**GPS: N43.09580 W0.03074**). From Lourdes take the D937 then D935 to Bagnères-de-Bigorre. Remain on the D935 out of Bagnères (the road to Tournay) and after 6km (3.7 miles) turn right onto the D938 to Barthe-de-Neste then Montréjeau (**GPS: N43.08400 E0.57189**). Come out on the D817 to St-Gaudens then all the way through to St-Martory, where you turn right onto the D117 and head down to St-Girons (**GPS: N42.98637 E1.14404**) and then Foix. Take the N20 out of Foix south to Tarascon-sur-Ariège (**GPS: N42.84569 E1.60199**).*

From Luz-St-Sauveur head out east on the D918 (again) on the slow ascent, initially, up to the Col du Tourmalet (**GPS: N42.90849 E0.14550**). The road surface is average here, and not particularly challenging until you get almost to the top where it gets very twisty for a short while. There is a nice café at Barèges on the way up, and another at the summit. As you ascend you'll notice to the north-east an observatory on top of a rocky outcrop which is at an altitude of 2872m. Col du Tourmalet is at 2115m, and one of the highest passes open to traffic in the region. It's part of the Tour de France route, and at the top there is a statue of a cyclist to commemorate the first Tour to pass through there in 1910. As usual, the views from the D918 as you climb up to, and from the top of the Col, are stunning on a clear day.

The descent down from the Col to Sainte-Marie-de-Campan along the Vallée de Campan is initially very twisty, but then gets much easier. It's lovely scenery all the way. At Sainte-Marie (**GPS: N42.98414 E0.22702**) turn right to remain on the D918 to the Col d'Aspin 13km (8 miles) away and then to Arreau. There are some hairpin bends just as you come out of the tiny village of Espiadet, and a number down to Arreau, but otherwise it's fairly straightforward. The Col d'Aspin is at 1489m and again offers superb views on a clear day of the surrounding area.

From Arreau take the D618 out heading east to Bagnères-de-Luchon, 32km (20 miles) away, via the Col de Peyresourde. This road has a good surface and, with some nice tight bends to keep it interesting, it's a thoroughly enjoyable ride. As you would

The beach at Vieux-Boucau-les-Baines

expect, the Col de Peyresourde at 1569m is spectacular. Bagnères-de-Luchon (**GPS: N42.79146 E0.59009**) is a spa town known for its thermal springs and baths. It sits on the confluence of the Rivers One and Pique, and is a good place for a break.

Take the main D125 out of Bagnères heading north to Fronsac, crossing over the River Garonne to rejoin the D618 to St-Girons, 60km (37 miles) away. This is a great road to ride on, not a fast one as there numerous bends, some very tight, and the road is quite narrow in places, but the overall scenery and the views are spectacular. The route passes through many small, pretty villages (with some very nice small cafés to stop for a break), and almost the entire 60km (37 miles) is through lovely forests and woodlands.

Remain on the D618 out of St-Girons all the way through to Tarascon-sur-Ariège, 56km (35 miles) to the east. As you come out of St-Girons the road goes along the Gorges de Ribaouto and the River Arac. The D618 section from St-Girons is a spectacular scenic ride. It's also a very challenging slow ride and great care is needed, particularly from the village of Massat to the Col de Port (1250m) and further on to just before Saurat, where the bends are extremely tight.

Tarascon-sur-Ariège straddles the River Ariège and is located just 17km (10.5 miles) south of Foix. It's a pretty, small town, and very busy during the summer months, and a good base for the next ride.

Day 6

This is the 171km (106 mile) ride going from France into the State of Andorra, then Spain, and finally back into France again! It's a lovely ride with high mountains, great scenery and good roads. But, as with all the previous days' rides, you really need good weather for this one!

*Alternative: leave Tarascon on the N20 (the road to Foix) coming off at Junction 12 to get on the D117 to Lavelanet and Quillan (**GPS: N42.87784 E2.18372**), 55km (34 miles) away. Leave Quillan on the D118 to Limoux and then Carcassonne. The distance from Tarascon to Carcassonne is 118km (73* *miles). The roads are predominately good with lots of wooded scenery.*

Leave Tarascon on the N20-E9 following the river to Les Cabannes and Ax-les-Thermes, where you continue due south, still on the N20, on the climb up to Andorra. At L'Hospitalet-prés-l'Andorra join the N22, where you enter a string of hairpin bends before it straightens out. From the N22 there are two options for entering Andorra. The first option is to go through the Envalira Tunnel, which was opened in 2002 to enable traffic to avoid the Port d'Envalira pass. The second option is to enter the country through the border control point on the outskirts of Pas de la Casa, and from there to ride along the Port d'Envalira Pass to join the main CG2 road to the capital, Andorra La Vella.

Pas de la Casa (**GPS: N42.54353 E1.73573**), at 2408m high, is a major modern ski resort with many duty-free shops. It's a good place to stop for a break if you decide not to take the tunnel route. The distance from Tarascon to the border control point at Pas de la Casa is 57km (35 miles).

Whichever option you go for, you eventually come out onto the CG2, and from there it's a mere 22km (13.6 miles) to the centre of Andorra La Vella (**GPS: N42.50709 E1.52586**). The capital city is at an altitude of 1409m, the highest in Europe, with a temperate climate of cold winters and warm summers. Apart from being a major ski resort, it has become a tax haven resulting in the development of a very modern banking system. The State is not a member of the EU, but the currency is the Euro, and a special customs arrangement is in place for citizens of the EU. There are dozens of good cafés and restaurants in the centre to choose from for lunch.

Leave Andorra La Vella on the CG1 following the River Valira to Sant Julià de Lòria, and from there cross the border into Spain onto the NA145 leading to La Seu d'Urgell (**GPS: N42.36355 E1.45580**). La Seu is an historic town, overlooked by the Sierra de Cadí Mountains, with a very attractive 11th century cathedral.

From La Seu it's a lovely ride east all the way along the N260 to the border crossing with France at Puigcerdà and Bourg-Madame (**GPS: N42.43373 E1.94086**). For most of this 48km (30 mile) ride the N260 follows close to the River El Segre, and the whole journey is very picturesque with some lovely bends.

After crossing back into France you're on the N116 out of Bourg-Madame to Saillagouse (**GPS: N42.45939 E2.03900**), which is only 9km (5.6 miles) away. If you have opted for the suggested Hôtel L'Ancienne Auberge at Bolquère, continue on the N116 for a further 8.8km (5.4 miles) then turn left onto the D10 for about 1.5 km (1 mile). The hotel is located just off the D10.

Bolquère, at 1640m, is set on the Cerdagne Plateau at the heart of the Parc Naturel Régional des Pyrénées. It is a very short distance from Super Bolquère to the north, and also very close to the popular linked ski areas of Font-Romeu and Pyrénées 2000. Font-Romeu (**GPS: N42.50499 E2.04088**) is one of the most popular winter sports locations in France, and one of the sunniest. In winter, the area has over 100km of marked trails for cross country skiers.

Day 7

The last day in the Pyrénées, the route takes you from Bolquère eastwards to the outskirts of Perpignan on the Mediterranean coast, then north to Narbonne, and from there to Carcassonne. The distance is around 204km (126 miles), of which 145km (90 miles) is on motorways and dual carriageways, a major contrast to previous days!

Leave Bolquère on the N116 descending to the outskirts of Perpignan, 85km (53 miles) to the east. The road follows the River Têt the whole way down. The first 22km (13.5 miles) down to the village of Olette is for the most part very twisty, with multiple bends in succession, but after that it's reasonably straight for most of the way, before the dual carriageway starts near Bouleternère. As usual, the ride until you reach the village of Prades (**GPS:** **N42.61558 E2.41837**) is very picturesque, with forests and woodland to both sides of the road, particularly through the Gorges de la Caranca.

A quick note here on the area. The region from Bolquère down to Perpignan is known as French Catalonia or Roussillon, and although there is no longer any strong separatist movement now, French Catalans have a strong sense of identity and the language is very much alive. Until the 1970's, Prades was a focus for Catalan resistance.

From Prades the scenery becomes less interesting, particularly when the N116 becomes a dual carriageway. At the end of the N116 follow the signs for the A9-E15 motorway, and join it northbound for 61km (38 miles) to Narbonne. If you want to visit Perpignan then join the D617 from the N116 and follow the signs for the centre. The gateway at Le Castillet is a good place to aim for (**GPS:** **N42.70090 E2.89421**).

Leave the A9 just to the south of Narbonne, and join the A61-E80 motorway heading west to Carcassonne. If you plan on staying at the suggested Hôtel Montmorency then leave the A61 at Junction 24 (Carcassonne-Est) and follow the D6113 to the Cité Médiévale.

Carcassonne is located in the Aude département of the Languedoc-Roussillon region. The real attraction is the old medieval Cité, and if you are staying at the Hôtel Montmorency you are almost outside the main gate/drawbridge at Porte Narbonnaise leading in. The Cité is surrounded by double stone walls with many impressive turrets, and inside are cobbled streets, numerous shops, cafés and restaurants. It's a major tourist attraction, and absolutely heaving in July and August. But it's worth the visit! If you are not staying at the hotel, parking is available almost outside the drawbridge at **GPS:** **N43.20657 E2.36661**.

Day 8

This is essentially the start of the three day ride back to the ferry terminal at Caen. The route for Day 8 goes up to Toulouse, then along to Castelsarrasin where you leave the motorway and go up-country to the overnight stop at Les Eyzies-de-Tayac-Sireuil in the Dordogne. It's about 316km (196 miles), half of which is on the A61 and A62 motorways. The prime reason for taking this route is to link up with the Périgord Noir (Black Périgord) tour of the southern Dordogne area (Tour 6), allowing you the option, time permitting, of spending a day or so there exploring the area before moving on.

Leave Carcassonne on the A61-E80 motorway to Toulouse, 95km (59 miles) away. The motorway takes you around the east side of the city to exit on the A62-E72 heading north to Bordeaux. Exit the motorway at Junction 9 (Castelsarrasin) onto the D813 for the short distance to Moissac.

Moissac, located in the Tarn-et-Garonne département in the Midi-Pyrénées region, is worth a stop. It's an attractive town with the River Tarn flowing through the centre. In 1930 this river flooded and much of the town was destroyed, however, the Saint-Pierre Abbey and its famous cloister and porch survived. The beautiful cloister with its marble columns and fine carvings are definitely worth viewing. The Abbey is located at **GPS:** **N44.10517 E1.08456**. There are a number of pleasant cafés in the square opposite the entrance.

Head out of Moissac on the D927 (to Lafrancaise) and after 11km (6.8 miles) turn left onto the D2, on up to Lauzerte then Montaigu-de-Quercy, 33km (20.5 miles) north. Montaigu is an exceptionally pretty market town on a hill top, with narrow streets, a 12th century Château, and many half-timbered medieval houses.

Come out of Montaigu on the D18 to Tournon-d'Agenais (nice Clock Tower and medieval ramparts here), through the town and out on the D102 to St-Vite. At the roundabout go straight ahead onto the D710 heading north to Belvès and then to the bridge across the River Dordogne at Siorac-en-Périgord. The distance from St-Vite to the bridge is 48km (30 miles). At Siorac take the D703 across the River Dordogne to Campagne and from here the D706 to Les Eyzies, 17km (10.5 miles) from the bridge.

(Note: the following paragraph on Les Eyzies is taken from Tour 6. If you intend staying several days exploring the Dordogne area then refer to that Tour and all the information provided under the heading 'What to do when you get there')

If you have opted to stay in Les Eyzies itself then the two main places to visit are all within walking distance. The village is very small, essentially a long high street, but it is very picturesque with high overhanging cliffs on one side and the River Vézère on the other. The area in and around Les Eyzies is historically very rich, and in the village itself (about half way along and partly built into the cliff face) is the Musée National de Préhistoire. Re-opened recently in a marvellous new state-of-the-art building (the museum used to be in the old castle at Les Eyzies) the exhibition is full of prehistoric remains and artefacts covering palaeolithic life, almost all found in the local area.

Day 9

This is the 292km (182 mile) ride north to the lovely town of Saumur in the Loire Valley. Leave Les Eyzies following the signs for Périgueux via the D47, D710 then N221. On the outskirts of Périgueux take the N21 all

Cité Médiévale, Carcassonne

the way up to Châlus (**GPS:** **N45.65495 E0.98172**), 61km (38 miles) north, before coming off onto the D901 to Rochechouart (**GPS:** **N45.82449 E0.82148**).

A quick historic note here on Châlus and Rochechouart. Châlus is dominated by the ruined Château de Châlus-Chabrol. It was here during a siege that Richard I (Richard the Lionheart) was killed by a French archer, Pierre Basile, in 1199 during a local rebellion. Rochechouart is a very pretty walled town and the site of a six billion tonne meteorite impact some 240 million years ago, thought to be the largest ever to hit the earth. There is very little evidence of this meteorite now, but some of the stone was used to build a number of the older buildings in the town, including another of Rochechouart's main attractions, the 13th century château on the edge of the town. Since 1832 the château has been the Town Hall (mairie) and also home to the Musée Départemental d'Art Contemporain. Before this, the château had remained in the hands of the de Rochechouart family for 800 years!

Leave Rochechouart on the D54 then D29 to Chabanais, continuing north from here to join the D948 to Confolens. Confolens (**GPS:** **N46.01400 E0.67175**) is beautiful with a long, narrow medieval bridge spanning the River Vienne, with very old houses on the hillside overlooking the town. The town is known worldwide for its annual International Folkore Festival held in August, where hundreds of thousands of people descend into the little town.

Continue on the D948 out of Confolens, onto the D148 then D741 out of Pressac all the way up to Poitiers, 62km (39 miles) north. Take the ring road N147 around Poitiers and then the very straight D347 to Loudun (**GPS:** **N46.99960 E0.08330**), Montreuil-Bellay and finally Saumur (**GPS:** **N47.27100 W0.08452** is the bridge over the River Loire). The distance from Poitiers to Saumur is about 90km (56 miles).

Day 10

The final day of the tour, and the ride back to the ferry terminal at Caen (Ouistreham), **GPS:** **N49.28304 W0.24934** is a straightforward ride and easy to navigate, covering some 236km (147 miles) across country which is about 4-4.5 hours riding. If you are catching the afternoon ferry back to Portsmouth you should ensure you leave no later than 09:30 hrs to allow time for fuel and break stops.

From Saumur take the D347 north to Longue-Jumelles, then the D938 to Baugé and La Flèche. At La Flèche join the D306, through Sablé-sur-Sarthe, where shortly afterwards the road becomes the D21 (this is the road to Laval). At the roundabout after the small village of St-Loup-du-Dorat (**GPS:** **N47.89233 W0.42278**), turn right onto the D24, a fast country road through Vaiges and Montsurs all the way to join the N162 leading into Mayenne (**GPS :** **N48.30577 W0.61721**). On arrival at Mayenne you will have ridden about 137km (85 miles) from Saumur.

Mayenne, located in the Pays de la Loire region, straddles the River Mayenne which passes through its centre. The town itself is steeped in history. Of particular note is its medieval castle, recently restored, and the excellent museum there. The surrounding area is also well known for its cider production. There are some pleasant cafés near the river which makes it a good place to have a break.

From Mayenne take the D23 then D962 through to Domfront (**GPS:** **N48.59167 W0.64849**), Flers and finally Condé-sur-Noireau, where the road number changes to the D562 all the way through to the Caen ring road. Join the N814 ring road bearing right, to go around anti-clockwise, and after about 5km (3 miles) you'll see the signs for the Ouistreham car ferry which will take you off the ring road and onto the D515/D514 leading to the terminal.

Suggested Places to Stay...

FONTENAY-LE-COMTE

HOTELS

Hôtel Fontarabie
57 rue de la République, 85200
Fontenay-le-Comte
Tel: +33 (0)2 51 69 17 24
Fax: +33 (0)2 51 51 02 73
Email: hotelfontarabie@wanadoo.fr
Web: www.hotel-fontarabie.com
GPS: **N46.46453 W0.80106**

Notes: Former post-house dating back to 1520. 49 rooms from €57. Located in the centre of the town. Own private car park.

Hôtel - Restaurant Le Rabelais
19 rue de l'Ouillette, Route de Parthenay,
85200 Fontenay-le-Comte
Tel: +33 (0)2 51 69 86 20
Fax: +33 (0)2 51 69 80 45
Email: hotel-lerabelais@wanadoo.fr
Web: www.hotel-lerabelais.com
GPS: **N46.46560 W0.79093**

Notes: Located close to the centre on the D745 as you come out of Fontenay to the north east. 54 rooms from €69. Private parking in an enclosed garage.

CAMPING

Camping La Joletière
85200 Mervent
Tel: +33 (0)2 51 00 26 87
Fax: +33 (0)2 51 00 27 55
Email: contact@campinglajoletiere.fr
Web: www.campinglajoletiere.fr/en/
GPS: **N46.52122 W0.77378**

Notes: Open 15th June to 15th September. Lovely location on the D99 in the Forêt de Mervent-Vouvant close to the lake just to the north of Fontenay-le-Comte. 73 pitches.

B&B

La Vallée
Xanton-Chassenon, 85240
St Hilaire de Loges
Tel: +33 (0)2 51 52 23 06
Mobile: +33 (0)6 98 28 42 25
Email: valgaffney@msn.com
Web: http://pagesperso-orange.fr/lavallee.bnb/
GPS: **N46.44128 W0.69266** (approx.)

Notes: Contact Pete and Val Gaffney. Very nice 19th Century restored mill offering four double rooms and one twin room, all with shower and WC. From €42. Open all year. Located 10km east of Fontenay-le-Comte, and 4km south of St Hilaire off the D15. English spoken.

BISCARROSSE

HOTELS

Hôtel Le Relais
216 Avenue du Maréchal Lyautey,
40600 Biscarrosse
Tel: +33 (0)5 58 78 10 46
Fax: +33 (0)5 58 78 09 71
Email: contact@hotel-le-relais.com
Web: www.hotel-lerelais.com
GPS: **N44.39266 W1.16464**

Notes: Located just off the D652 in the centre of the town. 24 fully equipped air conditioned rooms from €41. Own private car park.

Hôtel – Restaurant Les Vagues
99 rue des Iris, 40600 Biscarrosse-Plage
Tel: +33 (0)5 58 83 98 10
Fax: +33 (0)5 58 83 98 14
Email: contact@lesvagues.com
Web: www.lesvagues.com
GPS: **N44.45068 W1.24648**

Notes: Great location only 300m from a superb beach. 29 rooms from €54. Own private car park.

Continued...

CAMPING
Camping Campeole Plage Sud
40600 Biscarrosse-Plage
Tel: +33 (0)5 58 78 21 24
Fax: +33 (0)5 58 78 34 23
Email: plage-sud@campeole.com
Web: www.campeole.co.uk/LieuHebergement.aspx?lihe_id=9
GPS: **N44.44167 W1.24566**

Notes: Located just as you enter the town. At the roundabout take first exit off and follow the signs. Open from April to September. A very large site set amongst pine trees. Beach is 800m away. Good facilities.

Camping Campeole Le Vivier
40600 Biscarrosse-Plage
Tel: +33 (0)5 58 78 25 76
Fax: +33 (0)5 58 78 35 23
Email: vivier@campeole.com
Web: www.campeole.co.uk/LieuHebergement.aspx?lihe_id=4
GPS: **N44.45655 W1.24110**

Notes: Located to the north of the town. Open from April to September. A large site with good facilities, 800m from the beach.

VIEUX-BOUCAU

HOTEL
Hôtel La Côte d'Argent
Grande Rue, 40480 Vieux-Boucau-les-Baines
Tel: +33 (0)5 58 48 13 17
Fax: +33 (0)5 58 48 01 15
Email: hotel-cotedargent@wandadoo.fr
Web: www.lacotedargent-vieuxboucau.fr
GPS: **N43.78597 W1.40011**

Notes: Located right in the centre of the town. 36 rooms from €40, each with private bathroom, WC and a shower or bath. Private parking available at the rear of the hotel.

CAMPING
Airotel Le Vieux Port
Plage Sud, 40660 Messanges
Tel: +33 (0)1 76 76 70 00
Fax: +33 (0)5 58 48 01 69
Email: contact@levieuxport.com
Web: www.levieuxport.com
GPS: **N43.79768 W1.40016**

Notes: Located just off the D652, just to the north of Vieux-Boucau. It's well signposted from the roundabout by Super U. Open from Easter to 30th September. Just about the best campsite I've ever stayed at (many times). It's huge, but very spacious, with superb facilities and direct access to a fantastic beach. Great for surfing and relaxation.

B&B
A l'Orée de la Forêt
Lou Sarcelot, 40510 Seignosse
Tel: +33 (0)5 58 49 81 31
Email: info@loreedelaforet.com
Web: www.loreedelaforet.com
GPS: **N43.69389 W1.36846** (approx.)

Notes: Contact Pascal Froesch. Located just off the D337 near the lake Etang Noir. Open mid March to mid November. Beautiful property with five guest bedrooms sleeping two, three or four people. All bedrooms have a private bathroom. From €50.

L'accalmie
1295 Route d'Angresse, 40510 Seignosse
Tel: +33 (0)5 58 49 84 10
Mobile: +33 (0)6 72 24 82 43
Email: accalmie40@wanadoo.fr
Web: http://accalmie40.site.voila.fr
GPS: **N43.67138 W1.36688** (approx.)

Notes: Located to the south of Seignosse, just off the D652. Open all year. Modern house with three comfortable bedrooms, each with own shower room and WC.

LUZ-ST-SAUVEUR

HOTELS

Hôtel Le Montaigu
9 route de Vizos, Esquièze-Sère, 65120 Luz Saint Sauveur
Tel: +33 (0)5 62 92 81 71
Fax: +33 (0)5 62 92 94 11
Email: hotel.montaigu@wanadoo.fr
Web: www.hotelmontaigu.com
GPS: **N42.87492 W0.00090**

Notes: Located on the D172 just off the main D921 as you enter Luz-St-Sauveur. 42 rooms with WC and bath or shower. From €55. Private parking available.

Hotel Restaurant Les Templiers
6 place de la Comporte (Place de l"Eglise), 65120 Luz-St-Sauveur
Tel: +33 (0)5 62 92 81 52
Email: templiersluz@yahoo.fr
Webs: www.hotellestempliers.com
GPS: **N42.87191 W0.00318**

Notes: Nice location very close to the centre of the village just off the D921. Hotel is run by an English speaking French-Australian couple. 11 comfortable rooms from €45, all have a bathroom with shower, basin and WC (one room has a bath). Bikes can be parked down the side of the Hotel, not perfect but it's OK. They get a lot of bikers staying here.

CAMPING

Airotel Pyrénées Campsite
46 Avenue du Barege, 65120 Esquieze Sere (Luz-St-Sauveur)
Tel: +33 (0)5 62 92 89 18
Fax: +33 (0)5 62 92 96 50
Email: contact@airotel-pyrenees.com
Web: www.airotel-pyrenees.com/index.html
GPS: **N42.88031 W0.01117**

Notes: Located on the D921 on the left just before you reach the village of Luz-St-Sauveur. 99 touring pitches in 2.8 hectares. Altitude 700m. Good site and facilities. Site is not too high up if the weather is poor. Stayed here several times. English spoken.

B&B

Chambres d'hôtes Christine & Petxu
14 route de Villenave, 65120 Luz-St-Sauveur
Tel: +33 (0)5 62 92 90 79
Email: christinepetxu@orange.fr
Webs: www.chambres-hotes-luz.com
GPS: **N42.87233 W0.00033**

Notes: Contact Christine and Petxu Calderon. Four very comfortable guest rooms, one double and three twins.
All with shower or bathroom. From €45.

TARASCON

HOTELS

Hôtel Confort
3 Quai Armand Sylvestre, 09400 Tarascon-sur-Ariège
Tel: +33 (0)5 61 05 61 90
Fax: +33 (0)5 61 05 55 99
Email: contact@hotel-confort.fr
Web: www.hotel-confort.fr
GPS: **N42.84698 E1.60569**

Notes: Located just across the river from the centre, take first right. 14 rooms from €42. Private car park and garaging facilities available for motorbikes.

Hostellerie de la Poste
16 Avenue Victor-Pilhes, 09400 Tarascon-sur-Ariège
Tel: +33 (0)5 61 05 60 41
Fax: +33 (0)5 61 05 70 59
Email: info@hostellerieposte.com
Web: www.hostellerieposte.com
GPS: **N42.84810 E.160542**

Notes: Located next to the river just a little further on from the Hotel Confort above. 25 rooms all with WC and shower or bath from €44. Garage parking at extra cost available 400 metres from the hotel.
Book in advance if possible to Garage Chague +33 (0)5 34 09 00 31.

Continued...

CAMPING

Kawan Village Le Pré Lombard
BP 90148, 09400 Tarascon-sur-Ariège
Tel: +33 (0)5 61 05 61 94
Email: leprelombard@wanadoo.fr
Web: www.kawan-villages.com/en/camping/description-103-le-pre-lombard.html
GPS: **N42.84003 E1.61220**

Notes: Lovely location close to the River Ariège to the south east of the village. Very busy and lively site. 180 pitches in 3.5 hectares. Altitude 600m. Open from 4th March to 15th November. Excellent facilities.

Camping Le Malazéou
RN 20, 09110 Ax-les-Thermes
Tel: +33 (0)5 61 64 69 14
Fax: +33 (0)5 61 64 06 60
Web: www.campingmalazeou.com/uk/index.html
GPS: **N42.72879 E1.82575**

Notes: Located on the N20 just after Savignac-les-Ormeaux and before you come into Ax-les-Thermes. Site is open all year except November. Altitude of 700m. Good range of facilities.

B&B

Domaine Fournié
Route de Saurat, 09400 Tarascon-sur-Ariège
Tel: +33 (0) 5 61 05 54 52
Email: contact@domaine-fournie.com
Web: www.domaine-fournie.com
GPS: **N42.85570 E1.58454** (approx)

Notes: Contact Pierre Marie. Located just off the D618. 17th Century mansion offering three double rooms and two doubles, both with two single beds. From €45. All rooms have ensuite facilities.

Les Forges d'Enfalits
09400 Rabat-les-Trois-Siegneurs
Tel: +33 (0) 5 61 03 83 45 or +33 (0) 6 73 05 88 34
Email: enfalits@tiscali.fr
Web: www.forgesdenfalits.com
GPS: **N42.85582 E1.55551** (approx)

Notes: Contact Eric and Nathalie Pellerin. Located to the west of Tarasco. Stone house with five guest rooms comprising three doubles and two rooms with a double and two single beds. Each room has a private bathroom with shower and toilet. From €50.

BOLQUÈRE

HOTEL

Hôtel L'Ancienne Auberge
rue de L'Evêque, 66210 Bolquère
Tel: +33 (0) 4 68 30 09 51
Email: ancienne-auberge@aliceadsl.fr
Web: www.hotel-bolquere.com
GPS: **N42.50195 E2.07783**

Notes: Located just off the D10 from the centre of Bolquère. 14 rooms with shower or bath and WC. From €44. Parking and garaging available.

CAMPING

Huttopia Font-Romeu
Route de Mont Loius, 66120 Font-Romeu
Tel: +33 (0)4 68 30 09 32
Fax: +33 (0)4 68 04 56 39
Email: font-romeu@huttopia.com
Web: www.huttopia.com/en/Font-Romeu_font_romeu_campsite.html
GPS: **N42.50571 E2.04560**

Notes: Located just off the D618 just as you come out of Font-Romeu. 229 pitches in 7 hectares. Ensure the site is open before you arrive. Good modern facilities.

Camping Domaine Le Cerdan
11 chemin d"Estavar, 66800 Saillagouse
Tel: +33 (0)4 68 04 70 46
Email: lecerdan@lecerdan.com
Web: www.lecerdan.com
GPS: N42.46048 E2.03535 (approx.)

Notes: Located just off the N116 near the centre of Saillagouse. Altitude 1,300m. Closed in October. Nice site with good facilities.

B&B
Les Cariolettes
1 rue des Fontanilles, 66120 Font-Romeu-Odeillo
Tel: +33 (0)4 68 30 25 48
Mobile: +33 (0)6 83 59 29 38
Email: cariolettes@orange.fr
Web: www.gite-cariolettes.com
GPS: N42.49897 E2.03424

Notes: Located just off the D618 as you go through Odeillo. Turn right into rue des Lilas then first left. Renovated mountain farmhouse offering nine guest rooms with en-suite bathrooms. From €60.

CARCASSONNE

HOTEL
Hôtel Montmorency
2 rue Camille-Saint-Saëns, 11000 Carcassonne
Tel: +33 (0)4 68 11 96 70
Fax: +33 (0)4 68 11 96 79
Email: contact@lemontmorency.com
Web: www.lemontmorency.com/content
GPS: N43.20730 E2.36695

Notes: Off the D303 as you come in from the east off the A61. Superb location almost opposite the main entrance to the medieval city of Carcassonne. Highly recommend it, having stayed here many times. 20 rooms from €65. They have their own private car park (open), operated by a barrier. No restaurant, but the choice as you go into the old Cité is excellent.

CAMPING
Yelloh! Village Domaine d'Arnauteille
F11250 Montclar
Tel: +33 (0)4 68 26 84 53
Fax: +33 (0)4 68 26 91 10
Email: info@arnauteille.com
Web: www.camping-arnauteille.com
GPS: N43.12089 E2.28028 (approx.)

Notes: Located off the A61 motorway. At Carcassonne West turn off onto the D118 to Limoux, then after about 10km turn right onto the D43 to Montclar. Open from 20th March to 3rd October. 140 touring pitches available in 115 hectares. Excellent facilities.

Camping le Moulin de Sainte Anne
Chemin de Sainte-Anne, 11600 Villegly-en-Minervois
Tel: +33 (0)4 68 72 20 80
Fax: +33 (0)4 68 72 27 15
Email: campingstanne@wanadoo.fr
Web: www.moulindesainteanne.com
GPS: N43.28291 E2.44115

Notes: Located 12km to the north east of Carcassonne. Head north on the D620, just before the village of Villegly turn right onto the D435 (Chemin de St-Anne). Open from 1st March to 15th November. 45 touring pitches. Very good facilities.

B&B
Domaine des Castelles
11170 Caux et Sauzens
Tel: +33 (0)4 68 72 03 60
Fax: +33 (0)4 68 72 03 60
Web: www.bonadresse.com/languedoc-roussillon/gb_caux-et-sauzens.htm
GPS: N43.21850 E2.26044 (approx.)

Notes: Located near a small village to the west of Carcassonne, on the D48 (off the D119). Contact Isabelle Bretton. Former wine growing property offering three large guest rooms comprising one double bed and three singles; one double and one single bed, and one double bed. All rooms have shower rooms and toilet. From €65.

Continued...

La Maison sur la Colline
Mas de Sainte Croix, 11000 Carcassonne
Tel: +33 (0)4 68 47 57 94
Fax: +33 (0)4 68 47 58 67
Mobile: +33 (0)6 85 90 70 58
Email: contact@maisonsurlacolline.fr
Web: www.lamaisonsurlacolline.com
GPS: N43.19561 E2.376224 (approx.)

Notes: Contact Mrs Galinier. Open all year round. 5 bedrooms, all with private bathroom. English spoken. From €80.

LES EYZIES-DE-TAYAC

HOTELS

Hostellerie du Passeur
Place de la Mairie, 24620
Les Eyzies-de-Tayac
Tel: +33 (0)5 53 06 97 13
Fax: +33 (0)5 53 06 91 63
Email: contact@hostellerie-du-passeur.com
Web: http://www.hostellerie-du-passeur.com
GPS: N46.61944 E0.07445

Notes: 19 rooms from €80. Does not have a private car park as such, but there is plenty of space to put motorbikes in the front of the hotel. Have stayed here several times, once for 6 days, with no problems. Rooms are good, so is the restaurant. Superb location in the centre of Les Eyzies, and right by the River Vézère. English widely spoken by the staff.

Hôtel - Restaurant le Cro-Magnon
54 Avenue de la Préhistoire, 24620
Les Eyzies-de-Tayac
Tel: +33 (0)5 53 06 97 06
Fax: +33 (0)5 53 06 95 45
Email: hotel.cro.magnon.les-eyzies@wanadoo.fr
Web: www.hostellerie-cro-magnon.com
GPS: N44.93996 E1.00993

Notes: Located at the west end of the village just off the D47. 15 rooms from €80. Own private car park.

Hôtel des Roches
Avenue de la Forge, 24620
Les Eyzies-de-Tayac
Tel: +33 (0)5 53 06 96 59
Fax: +33 (0)5 53 06 95 54
Email: hotel@roches-les-eyzies.com
Web: www.roches-les-eyzies.com
GPS: N44.93498 E1.01769

Notes: Located on the D47 at the eastern end of the village. 41 rooms from €65. Own private car park. Good facilities provided.

CAMPING

Camping Le Paradis
24290 St-Léon-sur-Vézère
Tel: +33 (0)5 53 50 72 64
Fax: +33 (0)5 53 50 75 90
Email: le-paradis@perigord.com
Web: www.le-paradis.com
GPS: N45.00176 E1.07100

Notes: Opening season 1st April to 19th October. Located on the D706 about 10km (6.2 miles) north of Les Eyzies. This is a 5 star campsite and highly recommended. Run by a Dutch family, the setting on the River Vézère is superb. Facilities are excellent. Most staff are fluent in English.

B&B

Le Menestrel
1 rue de Laugerie, 24620
Le Eyzies-de-Tayac
Tel: +33 (0)5 53 04 58 94
Email: contact@menestrel-perigord.com
Web: www.menestrel-perigord.com
GPS: N44.94000 E1.00924

Notes: Open all year. Rooms from €55. Excellent location. Private car park.

SAUMUR

HOTEL
Hôtel Alcyon
2 bis, rue de Rouen, 49400 Saumur
Tel: +33 (0)2 41 67 51 25
Fax: +33 (0)2 41 51 34 85
Email: contact@alcyon-saumur.com
Web: http://www.alcyon-saumur.com
GPS: **N46.61944 E0.07445**

Notes: 17 rooms from €42. Secure and locked garage parking for motorbikes.

CAMPING
Kawan Village Ile d'Offard
Rue de Verden, Ile d'Offard, 49400 Saumur
Tel : +33 (0)2 41 40 30 00
Fax: +33 (0)2 41 67 37 81
Email: iledoffard@cvtloisirs.fr
Web: www.cvtloisirs.com
GPS: **N47.26009 W0.06510**

Notes: located on the Ile d'Offard, an island between both banks of the River Loire. Excellent, central location and well equipped site. Open from 1st March to 15th November. 208 touring pitches.

B&B
Ile du Saule Bed & Breakfast
Ile du Saule, 49400 Saumur
Tel: +33 (0)2 41 51 38 71
Web: www.iledusaule.com
GPS: **N47.26229 W0.06011** (approx.)

Notes: great place to stay, just off the D952 across from Ile d'Offard (it's not an island but a small peninsula off the D952). 3 rooms from €38. Private, safe parking. Owner speaks good English. Telephone only to book. Central location to the town. Look at the web site if you need convincing!

tour**extras:**
Touring Tips

• **Packing** - for keeping and organising clothes in my panniers I always use Eagle Creek Pack Cubes, again, available from Cotswold. These can be bought online at www.cotswoldoutdoor.com. They come in different sizes, but the most convenient one for clothes is the 10.5 litre capacity (26 x 35.5 x 6.5 cm). A zip around 3 sides of the Cube keeps your clothes securely inside, and with a mesh on the front you can easily see what's in each one. Take an additional empty one to put soiled clothing in. They are excellent! There is also one especially made for shoes. To maximise the available space always roll your clothes up where possible, particularly 'T' shirts, as it also helps to stop them becoming creased. Make sure that any liquids you take e.g. shower gel, shampoo etc. is wrapped up in protective plastic bags in case of a leak.

• **Ferries** - embarking and disembarking. The ramps leading into the ferry are often wet and can be very slippery, also the smooth deck itself once you are aboard, so take it nice and slowly. Opinions vary on this next point, but I always leave my bike on the side stand and in first gear, and I always stay and watch the Deckhand secure the bike to the deck to make sure it's done properly i.e. ensure that suitable padding is used across the saddle and the strap is ratched up tight. If you are not happy tell him.

• **Tank Bag** - not essential but extremely useful if you have one. They are ideal for putting a map and route directions/notes in if you're not using Sat/Nav, also for putting toll tickets and cash in, and all the little items you might use en route (glasses, water, camera, snack bars, phrase book etc.).

• **Fuel** - as in the UK it's widely available, but getting fuel on a Sunday, particularly in the more rural parts of France and away from the motorways, can be difficult. Most petrol stations are closed in France on a Sunday, and generally the only fuel available is from Supermarkets (some are open on Sunday mornings). The majority of supermarkets now have 24 hour self-service stations in which you can use a credit card with a pin number to get fuel. Most are modern and easy to use, with good instructions in English. However, you could have problems with some of the older ones, which may decline your card. If you find yourself in this situation and you desperately need fuel, wait until a local French person comes along and offer them cash to get some fuel from their pump - make sure it's the type of fuel you want. I have never had a problem getting fuel in this way as most locals understand the problem and are sympathetic. Supermarket fuel is almost always cheaper than from other petrol stations. It's now about the same price as in the UK.

• **Credit Card and Cash on the Bike** - I always take a third credit card with me and, together with €180, hide it in a secure place on the bike. This is for emergency use only and for peace of mind, in case I lose my wallet or it's stolen. Why €180? It will cover most immediate cash demands and if necessary will pay for two normal speeding fines of €90 each and save the hassle and embarrassment of being escorted to the cash point machine if I'm short of cash in my pocket! (Five years ago, half way across the

Pyrénées at Luz-St-Sauveur, I lost my cash, passport, driving license and two credit cards. But I had a third credit card hidden on the bike. It was a life saver!)

• **Travel and Breakdown Insurance** – is essential, so don't skip it. It can be very expensive to get your bike back to the UK if you breakdown and it can't be repaired locally.

• **Hotels** – when looking for suitable hotels to stay in before going on a trip I primarily go to two web sites, www.logis-de-france.fr/uk/index.htm and www.booking.com/. The Logis Group of hotels have over 3000 in Europe (most of them in France) and they are normally good value hotels in nice locations. If you contact their central reservation desk in Paris from the UK (**00 33 1 45 84 83 84**) you'll find they are able to talk to you in fluent English and booking is very easy. They can also call the hotel you are interested in direct and confirm whether, for example, secure parking or garaging is available for your bike. Booking.com offers a good choice in almost all locations and making reservations online is very easy. Their room rates are very competitive and often hard to beat. All hotel descriptions on the site will have information about the availability or otherwise of parking. The help desk is excellent if you have a problem or need help, and it's UK based (**0845 0805012**).

• **Mobile Phone -** unless you need to, switch off data roaming to avoid high roaming charges for email, MMS, web browsing etc. Wait until you can get Wi-Fi. A lot of hotels in France now have this facility, and it's widely available in public places. Also, in case you lose your mobile, have a written list of your most important telephone numbers (e.g. breakdown and travel insurance numbers etc.), and keep the list in a separate place away from your mobile.

• **First Aid Kit / Medical** – keep a small First Aid Kit handy at all times, either in your top box or tank bag. Also make sure you have some pain killers to hand and, not least of all, some Imodium Capsules to help stop diarrhoea (nothing worse when you're on a bike!).

• **Accommodation Booking details** – if you have pre-booked any or all of your accommodation make sure you have a duplicate copy of the booking form(s) packed separately, just in case you lose one. Again, nothing worse than arriving at your destination only to find that you can't remember where you're booked in! In addition to this, I also key into my mobile the telephone numbers of all the accommodation stops, which is also handy if you need to make a call to advise of a later than expected arrival.

• **Adapter Plugs** – essential to enable you to charge your mobile, camera, etc. If you don't have a couple then you should be able to buy them from the shop on the ferry.

• **Michelin Maps** – the best available! Folded one for general planning, the bigger spiro-bound one for the detailed stuff, heavy but worth it's weight in gold!

• **Helmet** – unless your bike is visible, or you can put it in your top box, it's not advisable to lock your helmet onto the bike and walk away. They're too easy to nick, and if it does go you're stuffed until you can get a replacement. It's just not worth it.

• **When riding**, always, always, always keep your documentation, mobile, credit card(s), cash etc. in the same places on your jacket and trousers or bike. Don't change the locations. It makes items easy to find and check on, and goes a long way to preventing those panicky, heart-stopping moments when you have that awful feeling that you might have lost or left something behind in that last café you stopped off at!

• **Finally** – It's mentioned elsewhere in this book, but just a reminder that a lot of the road numbers in France are currently changing, so have to mind the main towns on your route and you should be OK. All the Tours in this book have been updated to the latest road numbers available at the time, but a few could easily have changed subsequently.

tourextras:
To Do & Packing Lists

TO DO LIST *(see notes also)*
- Phone Credit Card Company(s)
- Buy Euros
- Bike Service
- Top-up Scottoiler
- Clean Bike
- Charge Batteries - Mobile, Camera etc.
- Check for Sat/Nav Software Updates
- Route(s) download to GPS unit
- Phone Bike Insurance Company
- Check Passport validity
- Check Breakdown & Travel Insurance
- Credit Card & Cash on Bike

DOCUMENTS
- Passport
- Driving License (both parts)
- Bike Insurance Certificate
- Vehicle Registration Document (V5)
- MOT Certificate
- Travel Insurance
- Breakdown Insurance
- European Health Insurance Card (EHIC)
- Denplan Card & Emergency Tel.No.
- Accommodation Booking Details
- Ferry Ticket(s)
- Important Telephone Nos. (written)

MAIN PACKING LIST
- Michelin Map of France (folded)
- Michelin Map of France (spiro-bound)
- Alan Rogers Camp Site Guide
- Pocket French Phrase Book
- Euros & Credit Card(s)
- French Adapter Plugs (2)
- Camera & Battery Charger
- Mobile Phone & Charger
- Snack Bars
- Paperback
- Sun & Reading Glasses
- Water Bottle (for top-box)
- Multi-Tool Kit
- Toilet Bag (Razor, Toothbrush etc.)
- T shirts, Shirts, Trousers/Jeans
- Socks, Pants, Sweater
- Waterproof Anorak
- Shoes / Trainers
- Small Sewing Kit

MEDICAL
- Small First Aid Kit
- Paracetemol/Asparin
- Imodium Capsules
- Sun Cream
- Insect Repellent

CAMPING LIST *(see notes also)*
- Tent
- Sleeping Bag
- Air Bed / Mattress
- Pillow (blow-up)
- Gas Stove & Gas Cylinder
- Lighter
- Torch
- Cutlery
- Rubber Mallet
- Tea Towel
- Tea, Coffee, Sugar, Powdered Milk
- Mug, Bowl, Plate, Kettle, Cooking Pan
- Dishcloth / Pan Scrubber
- Pre-Packed Meals
- Washing-up Liquid
- Small Tent Lamp
- Soap (all purpose)
- Trek Towel

tourextras:
Notes on To Do & Camping Lists

If you use lists then you're unlikely to forget anything of importance. Keep them up-to-date! The lists in this book are the ones I personally use, and most of the items on them will be applicable to the majority of bikers travelling abroad, but adapt them where necessary to suit your own circumstances.

NOTES ON THE TO DO LIST

• **Phone up Credit Card Company** - tell them the dates you are going to be away so that your card is marked accordingly on their computer system. If you don't do this you may have problems, at least initially, in using the card because of the security checks that may have to be done. Give them a mobile number they can call you on, and make sure you have theirs in case it gets lost or stolen.

• **Buy Euros** - have a 100 or so for day to day use, and top-up from a cash point when running low.

• **Bike Service** - if needed. Otherwise, check everything yourself as much as you are able to, including fluid levels, tyre pressures, and whether there is sufficient legal tread for the duration of your trip. Bike tyres are more expensive in France.

• **Check for Sat/Nav software updates** - for your GPS Unit

• **Computer Route(s) download to GPS Unit** - if you have Sat/Nav and want to plan your routes beforehand on your PC.

• **Phone Bike Insurance Company** - if you are obliged to tell them that you are taking the bike abroad.

•**Credit Card & Cash on Bike** - see under Touring Tips for more information on this.

NOTES ON THE CAMPING LIST

Camping is great fun when touring on a motorbike, providing the weather is good! It's also a cheaper and more flexible option than staying in hotels and B&B's. The camping list provided gives a good indication of the main items you'll need to take, but much ultimately depends on how much you want to do.

Obviously, you'll need a small, lightweight and compact tent, also a sleeping bag which will roll up into a small bag. These are widely available now and not very expensive.

If you plan on cooking for yourself then you'll need to take at least everything on the list. For a gas stove I use a Coleman Outlander® which is brilliant, has a very handy self-igniting switch, and folds down to fit nicely into a small compact bag. The unit is very easy to use and simply screws into a small Coleman self-sealing 250 gas container.

Put tea, coffee, sugar, powdered milk, and washing-up liquid in Nalgene (or similar) leak proof cylindrical containers. You can buy these online from Cotswold Outdoor www.cotswoldoutdoor.com which is where I have bought almost all my camping and travel gear over the years. I also take with me a few pre-packed meals produced by Wayfayrer (place foil pouch in boiling water) or TravelLunch (add hot water) which you can also buy from Cotswold. They are surprisingly tasty, and a quick and easy way to grab a meal if you're on an isolated campsite or arrive late and everything is closed.

Of course, you could opt to just take the camping basics and forget the cooking side of things by going only to larger campsites with good facilities i.e. café / restaurant or take-away on site, or camping close to a village with similar offerings.

Two final items worthy of mention on the camping list are liquid soap and towel, both produced by Lifeventure®. I always take with me a 200ml bottle of their concentrated all purpose soap, because you can use it to have a shower, wash your hands, wash fruit, and even your clothes. It's a brilliant product with an anti-bacterial action, and a bottle of it seems to last a long time. For a towel I use their soft fibre Trek Towel (get an XL one), which folds up into a small, compact zipped pouch. It's amazingly absorbent, quick to dry, and ideal for when you have a shower.

When travelling solo on the bike in France I put all my camping gear in a strong, Ortlieb waterproof bag. You can buy these in a range of different sizes and they are perfect for the job. I wedge it up against the top box where the pillion passenger would sit and secure it to the bike with 3 bungee straps. Note: I often take this bag with me on short trips away instead of the side panniers if I'm not camping. If nothing else it makes filtering a lot easier!

tourextras:

Useful Information while travelling in France

TIME DIFFERENCE

GMT + 1 hour

CURRENCY

Euro € divided into 100 cents. There are 8 coins – 1, 2, 5, 10, 20 and 50 cents, and €1 and €2. The notes are €5, €10, €20, €50, €100, €200 and €500.

ELECTRICITY

220 volts AC, 50Hz

HOLIDAYS

The French generally take their holidays in July and August so most inland parts of France will be quiet at this time. Coastal areas, particularly in the South of France

ROAD SIGNS

Many road signs will be familiar or obvious. The main ones you'll come across are listed below :

ACOUTEMENT NON STABILISE :	Soft / unstable verges
ALLUMEZ VOS FEUX:	Turn on your lights
ARRÊT:	Stop
ARRÊT INTERDIT:	No stopping
ATTENTION AU FEU:	Fire Hazard
ATTENTION TRAVAUX:	Roadworks
CÉDEZ LE PASSAGE:	Give way
CHAUSSÉE DEFORMER:	Uneven surface
CHAUSSÉE GLISSANTE:	Road is slippery
DOUANE:	Customs
FIN DE CHANTIER:	End of roadworks
GRAVILLONS:	Loose chippings
LA BANDE D'ARRÊT D'URGENCE:	Emergency lane
LA DÉVIATION :	Diversion
LE DÉPASSEMENT:	Overtake
LE PÉAGE:	Pay Toll
LE SENS INTERDIT:	No entry
LE SENS UNIQUE:	One Way
PASSAGE PIÉTONS:	Pedestrian crossing
RALENTIR:	Slowdown
RAPPEL:	Remember (usually to remind you of a speed limit)
ROUTE BARREE:	Road closed
SERREZ À DROITE:	Keep to the right
VOUS N'AVEZ PAS LA PRIORITÉ:	You do not have priority / give way

USEFUL PHRASES / WORDS

Take a pocket French phrase book with you when you go and keep it in your jacket pocket. Below are some of the more helpful words and phrases:

Hello	Bonjour
Good evening	Bonsoir
Goodbye	Au revoir
Yes	Oui
No	Non
Please	S'il vous plaît
Thank you	Merci
Excuse me	Pardon
Left	la gauche
Right	le droit
Can you help me please	Aidez moi s'il vous plaît
I do not speak French	Je ne parle pas français ...
I don't know how to say it in French	Je ne sais pas le dire en français
Do you speak English?	Parlez vous Anglais?
I don't understand	Je ne comprends pas
I understand a little	Je comprends un peu
Can I pay by credit card?	Puis-je payer avec le carte de credit?
It's straight ahead	C'est tout droit
Turn left	Tournez à gauche
Turn right	Tournez à droite
Where is the?	Où est le?
How far is it?	C'est à quelle distance?
The menu please	Le menu, s'il vous plait
A large white coffee please	Une crême grande s'il vous plait
A large black coffee please	Une café noir grande s'il vous plait
An expresso coffee please	Une café s'il vous plaît
An expresso coffee with milk please	Une café au lait s'il vous plaît
The bill please	L'addition s'il vous plait
Where is…	Où est…
My name is…	Je m'appelle…
Where is the nearest petrol station?	Où se trouve la station service la plus proche?
I have a reservation	J'ai une réservation
I would like a room	Je voudrais une chamber
for one night / two nights	our une nuit / deux nuits
for one person / two people	pour une personne / deux personnes
with two beds	à deux lits
How much is this?	C'est combien?

will be extremely busy and the major routes towards the coast will be busier than normal.

FUEL
Unleaded Super 95/98 is "Essence sans Plomb". Diesel is "Gazole or Gas-oil".

RIDING ETIQUETTE
Bikers are far more welcome in France than in the UK, and are given considerable respect and courtesy on the roads. Motorcyclists coming in the opposite direction will invariably lift their left hand slightly as a 'hello' gesture. A slightly outstretched right leg means 'thanks', frequently used by bikers when a motorist has made an overtake much easier by moving closer to the kerb.

TIPPING
A 15% tip is generally expected if a service charge has not been included in your bill. However, most hotels and restaurants include this automatically, so check your bill. It is customary to tip most service staff, including cloakroom attendants, guides and taxi drivers.

SHOPS
You will find that most shops and hypermarkets are closed on Sundays and many (except some large hypermarkets) will close for lunch at around midday, sometimes for two hours on all other days.

THE LEGAL STUFF

RIDING
In France, you ride on the right hand side. An obvious statement, but you can easily forget, especially when pulling out from service stations or side roads, in particular those on the left hand side.

RADAR DETECTORS
Radar detectors are illegal in France.

HELMETS
As in the UK, a helmet must always be worn by the rider and pillion passenger.

GB STICKERS
If your number plate does not have the EU marking on it (which is accepted in all EU countries), you will need to put a GB sticker on or close to your number plate.

HEADLIGHTS / BULBS
In France, it is compulsory to have dipped headlights on during the day and to carry a spare set of bulbs.

INSURANCE
Check that your insurance policy covers you, and a pillion (if applicable), for riding in France. In France you must carry your insurance certificate with you at all times.

DOCUMENTATION
The following original documentation (not copies) should ALWAYS be carried. If you are stopped by the police, show these documents as soon as possible :

- Driving Licence
- Passport (if your driving licence does not include a photograph)
- Vehicle Registration Document (V5)
- Motor Insurance Certificate

If the bike is not registered in your name, you should carry a photocopy of the registration document and a signed letter from the owner, which gives you permission to ride the vehicle in France.

European Health Insurance Card (EHIC)
This replaced the old Form E111, which ceased to be valid from 1st January 2006. It is not the law to have an EHIC, but you shouldn't go to any EU country without one. Should you require emergency medical treatment, this card will enable you to obtain

reduced or sometimes free treatment. If you already have one, make sure it's not going to expire when you're over there. Note that there are restrictions in place so it is best to check at http://www.ehic.org/

Also note, that some medical insurance policies will be void if do not have the above card. You can pick up a form from the Post Office or very easily apply online at http://www.ehic.org/apply.html

SPEEDING & SPEED LIMITS

Speeding offences will often incur on the spot fines so it is a good idea to have some Euros handy. The majority of fines are usually €90, but if you exceed a limit by a considerable margin then the fine can be astronomical, and you run the real risk of being arrested and having your bike impounded. If an official receipt for payment is not automatically given to you then ask for one. If you don't have sufficient cash on you then you'll be escorted to the nearest cash machine!
Speed limits are indicated in kilometres per hour (kph) and you may find it useful to mark your speedo before you set off with the kph equivalent if it isn't indicated already. Unless otherwise signposted, limits are as follows :

Built up areas: 50kph (31mph)
Villages: 70kph (43mph)
Open roads: 90kph (56mph), sometimes 70kph (43mph) if indicated.
Dual carriageways: 110kph (68mph) 100kph (62mph) when wet.
Toll roads & Motorways (péage): 130kph (80mph) or 110kph (69mph) if wet.

There are exceptions to the rules. All limits except the 50kph limit are reduced by 10 kph in the rain, and if it is foggy or heavy rain with visibility reduced to 50 metres, a speed limit of 50kph will apply to all roads. Toll road speed limits can fluctuate according to driving conditions and circumstances.
On more rural roads, speed limits will sometimes appear on a sign with the village name on it, if it is different to the normal 50kph. If there is no speed limit indicated then it is 50kph once you are past the sign. On leaving, the village sign will have a red line through it, which also indicates the end of the speed restriction unless there is a sign to say otherwise.

AUTOROUTES / TOLLS

On approaching a toll booth, keep to the right because these are normally manned, unless stated otherwise. Some booths will have signs for motorcycles either prohibiting or directing you. You may even be exempt from paying at certain times of the year, for instance on some race weekends.
If you are riding in a group, go through the barrier one at a time. Each bike will need a ticket. Each bike must go under the barrier and clear the sensor allowing the barrier to drop before the next bike goes through.
Note: it is an offence to run out of fuel on an Autoroute. If you find yourself in this situation, it would be prudent to put it down to some mechanical failure if you're spotted!

DRINKING & DRIVING

Don't do it! Limits are much lower than in the UK. The legal limit is 0.05 percent. If you are found over the limit, you will get a fine or worse still, you may be imprisoned.

ROAD SIGNS

Priorité à droite (meaning priority is to the right).
If you are on any road with other roads joining from the right, beware as these road users may have priority over you and they can and will pull out without looking. Here are the priorité à droite signs that you need to be aware of and look out for when travelling on any French road.

The main sign you need to be aware of in France is the Priorité à droite sign. Unique to France, it simply means that priority is to the right at the NEXT junction, whether a crossroads, side road, etc. There will be no road markings indicating the junction and the junction should be within 100 to 150 metres of the sign.

It is essential that you give way to any traffic entering the road from the right. If you were to have a collision, you would be at fault and liable.

Don't be surprised when changing from a minor road to a major road, traffic on the major route giving way to you.

All that said, the French are extremely bike-friendly and will often give way anyway, whatever the situation.

This sign is the exact opposite of the above and advises you that at the next junction, once again, not necessarily a crossroads, you (being the main road user) have priority. The minor roads will be marked accordingly and will have Give Way signs (CEDEZ LE PASSAGE) or an octagonal STOP sign.

You will often see this sign at the entrance to a town. From this point onwards, the priorité à droite rule applies at ALL junctions. This system is becoming increasingly common as it seems to be an effective way of calming traffic and making road-users more junction aware. You must keep a good look-out for this sign and 'give way to traffic entering from the right'.

This sign is the opposite of the above and will appear on main roads exiting a town. The sign indicates that from that point on, priority is given to the main road traffic, until you see the End Priority sign with the black diagonal bar through.

Just to confuse things even more, there are exceptions to the priorité à droite rule, namely at Roundabouts. Most have familiar priorities, such as Give Way signs at entrances.

Another important road sign in France is the STOP sign. It's a very obvious sign but in France, as in the UK, a STOP sign really does mean stop! If your bike does not come to a complete halt, you could face an on the spot fine if caught.

Roundabouts

Roundabouts can be confusing in France. If you see a sign stating "Vous n'avez pas la priorité" or "Cédez le passage", priority is given to vehicles on the roundabout. If there is no sign, priority is given to traffic entering the roundabouts. Remember, vehicles will be coming around from the left!

USEFUL CONTACTS

British Embassy & Consulars

(http://ukinfrance.fco.gov.uk/en/)

Paris area :	00 33 (0) 1 44 51 31 00
Bordeaux area :	00 33 (0) 5 57 22 21 10
Lille area :	00 33 (0) 3 20 12 82 72
Lyon area :	00 33 (0) 4 72 77 81 78
Marseille area :	00 33 (0) 4 91 15 72 10

Emergency Services

Dial 112 from a mobile phone. This will connect you to the emergency switchboard for your area.

tourextras:
Selected Ferry Operators between UK & France

Operator	From	To	Frequency	Sailing time	Telephone	Operator Website
Britanny Ferries	Poole	Cherbourg	17 weekly	4 hr 15 mins	0871 244 0744	www.brittany-ferries.co.uk
Brittany Ferries	Portsmouth	Caen	3 daily	6 hr 00 min	0871 244 0744	www.brittany-ferries.co.uk
Brittany Ferries	Portsmouth	Cherbourg	7 weekly	3 hr 00 min	0871 244 0744	www.brittany-ferries.co.uk
LD Lines	Dover	Boulogne	16 weekly	1 hr 45 min	0844 576 8836	www.ldlines.co.uk
P&O Ferries	Dover	Calais	up to 25 daily	1 hr 30 min	08716 645 645	www.poferries.com
Seafrance	Dover	Calais	up to 15 daily	1 hr 15 min	0871 22 22 500	www.seafrance.com
LD Lines	Dover	Dieppe	6 weekly	4 hr 15 min	0844 576 8836	www.ldlines.co.uk
Norfolk Line	Dover	Dunkerque	11 daily	2 hr 00 min	0844 847 5042	www.norfolkline.com
Eurotunnel	Folkestone	Calais	up to 35 daily	0 hr 35 min	08705 35 35 35	www.eurotunnel.com
Transmanche	Newhaven	Dieppe	14 weekly	4 hr 00 min	0800 917 1201	www.transmancheferries.com
Britanny Ferries	Plymouth	Roscoff	8 weekly	5 hr 30 min	0871 244 0744	www.brittany-ferries.co.uk
Condor Ferries	Poole	St Malo	5 weekly	4 hr 35 mins	0845 609 1024	www.condorferries.co.uk
LD Lines	Portsmouth	Le Havre	13 weekly	5 hr 30 min	0844 576 8836	www.ldlines.co.uk
Brittany Ferries	Portsmouth	St Malo	7 weekly	10 hr 00 min	0871 244 0744	www.brittany-ferries.co.uk